# Mathematics for Children with Severe and Profound Learning Difficulties

# LES STAVES

**David Fulton Publishers**

London

**Dedication**

Some calendars have snippets of wisdom printed on them, one day my calendar said to me

'Every adult needs a child to teach; it's the way that adults learn.'

I would like to dedicate this book to all the children who have taught me how to teach over the past thirty years.

I would like to thank Wendy for her patience and love.
Graheme Lauder for being a friendly critical reader.
Sue Bainbridge and Flo Longhorn in their different ways for encouraging a beginner.

David Fulton Publishers Ltd
Ormond House, 26–27 Boswell Street, London WC1N 3JZ

www.fultonpublishers.co.uk

First published in Great Britain by David Fulton Publishers 2001

*British Library Cataloguing in Publication Data*
A catalogue record for this book is available from the British Library

ISBN 1–85346–695–6

The publishers would like to thank John Cox for copy-editing and Sally Critchlow for proofreading this book

Typeset by Mark Heslington, Scarborough, North Yorkshire
Printed in Great Britain by Bell & Bain Ltd, Glasgow

# Contents

# Introduction

### Fundamental things apply

This book is mostly about the learning upon which our understanding of mathematics is built. Parts One to Three examine in detail how children evolve knowledge, skills and processes that they require to move towards numeracy. Though it explores parts of learning that are often taken for granted, hopefully readers will find that we should take nothing for granted because close examination of fundamental learning reveals fascinating detail and points our thoughts towards many useful avenues for teaching special pupils, who are developing their essential sense of mathematics and learning to use it. Part Four of the book explores issues related to the mathematics curriculum for special pupils including the nature of progress, the interplay between the National Curriculum, the 2001 guidelines, P levels and the National Numeracy Strategy.

The new National Curriculum challenges us to ensure that there is one curriculum for all pupils. It empowers us to modify our approaches to ensure that that there is a continuum of learning upon which all children can find their appropriate place and progress, consolidate, or maintain their learning. This is of major importance where children of different abilities learn together. Flexibility to do this is a major theme in the new guidelines issued by the QCA[1] in 2001.

The introduction of the National Numeracy Strategy has prompted us to take a fresh look at the teaching of mathematics to pupils with very special needs. The introduction of P levels has paved the way for acknowledgement that there is a lot of mathematical learning that takes place before Level 1 of the National Curriculum. Though the P levels themselves are bare outlines, there is a rich seam of fundamental strategies and experiences to be offered to pupils, and this book discusses how P levels can be enhanced. The framework of the Numeracy Strategy, or the content of Programmes of Study may seem to refer to complex mathematics but beneath that complexity there are essential elements of learning. Appropriate interpretation of the framework focuses on the elements that are relevant to the needs of our special pupils. If my book gives teachers encouragement when they recognise that it often echoes the quality of their own teaching, I will be well pleased. I hope that it will stimulate you to devise many more exciting ways to involve your children in the mathematics that surrounds them.

Remember, mathematics is not only your useful servant it also represents integral rhythms in our lives.

---

[1] QCA (2001) Planning, Teaching and Assessing the Curriculum for Pupils with Learning Difficulties. Sudbury: QCA.

# Part One

# Mathematics in daily life

# 1 The significance of mathematics

In his Royal Institute Christmas Lecture in 1997 professor of mathematics Ian Stewart emphasised, 'The mathematical mind is rooted in the human visual, tactile and motor systems. Counting is based on touch and movement, geometry is visual'.

In the Goon Show Moriarty asked 'How are you with Mathematics?' and Secombe replied, 'I speak it like a native'. Mathematics is a language we all speak, it is a medium that enables us to observe and share information about our surroundings and occurrences. This book is about how we promote these processes for children who are learning at early stages of development. When regarded as an academic subject, with a leaning towards abstraction and calculation, the relevance of mathematics to such pupils seems marginal. However, mathematics is intrinsically woven into our life and language. In fact the basic concepts of mathematics are so natural to us they are part of the thinking we do even before we speak. The part that mathematical thinking plays in our intuitive reasoning is very important to our conscious functions and appreciation of life. There is a great deal of mathematical learning that takes place before children start school. By that time most children have developed intuitive concepts relating to space and quantity that are the bedrock of their later ability to use the symbolic and abstract aspects of mathematical expression. It is interesting to note that Einstein described his creative mathematical thinking as, 'Initially involving visual and muscular processes'. He infers that his thinking had sensory roots and said that words and other signs that could be used to try to describe his feelings only came into use after the initial associative play. What better witness could we have to testify that mathematical understanding has physical and sensory origins and mathematical learning is built upon a wider foundation than logic alone?

The fundamental sense of mathematics begins long before we can talk numbers, and there is much to the natural course of learning mathematics before counting; exploring this part of mathematics is very important for children who are at fundamental stages of learning.

Some people may suggest that subject teaching is inappropriate for children who are at early levels of development, because the nature of early learning is the same in all subjects. But at even the most fundamental levels of learning many activities that children participate in do have distinct associations to specific subjects, they relate to distinctive content, distinct language and ways of thinking. For example, in the

1

process of sharing the experience of reading with an adult, a young child experiences turn taking, visual discrimination, matching symbols to sounds, etc. The same skills would be exercised in the course of playing a dice or number game together, but the two activities have different purposes and flavours. In the reading activity a story emerges, the purpose of the communications, discriminations, and sound matching is to reveal a thread that includes descriptions of circumstances, questions of intent and social interaction. Whereas in the number game as the dice rolls the children use the same skills to be aware of changing quantities, the suspense of comparisons, using number labels, comparisons of size, frequencies. So while the same tools and skills are being used, there is something distinctive about the ways of thinking that are being promoted (Grove and Peacy 1999). On the one hand there is the purpose of literature, and on the other the purpose of mathematics, and these different experiences engender distinctly different 'Ways of knowing', it is these distinctly different styles that define the spirits of the subjects (Wragg 1997). So the child is using the same tools and skills in different contexts, and these contexts give the process of learning breadth and real life relevance. When children experience these different purposes and flavours they learn about the existence of different aspects of life, all of which are important to them. Figure 1.1 summarises ways that mathematics contributes to the everyday quality of our lives.

---

**Mathematics is**

- **Important to communication**
  Its language expresses the nature and order of things, we cannot live without descriptions of quantities, space and time.

- **Important in our practical lives**
  Its concepts are the basis of many of our practical skills.

- **Important in helping us understand relationships**
  We use it to describe and compare things, all its parts are interrelated, e.g. addition and subtraction; its concepts help us understand the world around us.

- **Important because it helps us be systematic**
  With its structures and tools we can record, bring order and remember our observations. Its patterns and rules help us recognise what we know, and predict what might happen.

- **Important because it is a tool for our imagination**
  We express ourselves and are emotionally affected by its patterns, they affect us in music, movement, the visual and tactile arts. A waltz feels different to rock and roll.

- **Important because it fascinates us**
  Even though many people fear abstract mathematical language and processes, they are fascinated by patterns, comparisons, changes to quantities, etc. and are interested in anticipating and predicting outcomes.

**Figure 1.1**  Ways in which mathematics is important to our lives

# 2 How mathematical learning begins

## The natural and cultural roots of mathematics

Introducing number sense, our natural inclination to notice the numerous – a neurological dimension

Mathematics has been placed upon a pedestal as a realm of abstract intellectual thought. For many years philosophers and psychologists have suggested that mathematical knowledge was the result of the development of logic, and children could not learn it until they were capable of logical thought (Piaget 1965). Recently writers who are interested in the functions of different parts of the brain have paid attention to how mathematical knowledge begins. They have suggested that we are born with areas of the brain that specialise in the recognition of 'numerosity', i.e. the perception of quantities. Both Brian Butterworth (1999) and Stanislas Dehaene (1997) have written books that survey the beginnings of mathematical thinking, and the practices of counting, recording and calculation from pre history to modern times. Through these histories and by relating them to the observations and case studies of psychologists and neuro-scientists, they illustrate that at birth we possess a fundamental 'sense of number' that enables us to compare and select the larger of two groups. From these early abilities we quickly learn to have a sense of their order by size. Butterworth calls the brain circuitry that provides these processes 'The Number Module'. He suggests that children use it to develop elementary ideas about quantities and numbers from information they gather through their physical senses and cultural experiences. This is the fundamental beginning of understanding numeracy; without it we would not be able to lead our practical daily lives, nor would mathematics ever fly to its abstract heights.

Models connecting early learning to sensory activity are not new or unique to mathematics. What is fresh and especially interesting for us in Butterworth's suggestions is the idea of a number module, drawing direct information from touch, sight and sound to extend a sense of number. This is perhaps somewhat akin to the way that we have previously envisaged a sense of colour – we readily accept that children can recognise and match colours before they can name them.

We will return to number sense in a later chapter. It is important for children with very special needs because it relates to learning that is so deep-seated that we take it so much for granted that it has not been part of our curriculum.

## Counting – a practical and psychological dimension

As I have mentioned earlier, up to the 1960s psychologists proposed that the development of mathematical knowledge first required the development of logical, abstract thought. Piaget (1965) considered young children's abilities to learn and recite number sequences and arithmetic facts as simple meaningless acts. More recently research has shown that number concepts and the use of meaningful counting actually interact to enable the child to construct more sophisticated concepts of number, and form the basis of understanding practical and arithmetical operations. There has been increasing interest by psychologists in how children actually learn to count. Though it is an ability that many children master before they attend school, it has been shown to be a complex skill, with many parts. Counting forms the basis of practical mathematics and arithmetic and even the abstract realms of mathematics are dependent upon it. Learning to count is learning to extend the power of your number module. Young children learn it so instinctively that guidance in the National Curriculum only skims over it. Working with children who have difficulties learning to count requires us to know a great deal more about its parts, and, as with number sense, we will return to them after we have considered the background relating to the tools and processes that our children use to learn.

## Personal and social mathematics

Learning is driven by curiosity. It begins as children explore with their senses. Initially they respond to basic drives to satisfy hunger and other essential needs by reflexive reactions to external sounds and other stimuli, by looking and reaching, etc. Though these processes help them to establish their early relations with other people, they also focus a great deal on exploration that involves absorbing perceptual experiences of a very localised environment. This includes the close examination of their own bodies and hands; though they are not necessarily inclined to share such exploration with others. They realise significant things about their observations and develop ideas which they begin to generalise. They are drawn into communication as they encounter others; they respond, communicating both about the notions they have developed and the questions that their ideas and curiosity raise. The processes of these stages spiral forward like waves, depicted in Figure 2.1 There is repeated feedback and progression as personal exploration results in

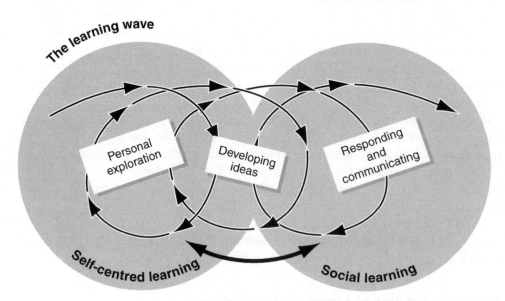

Personal exploration, response and communication generate social learning

**Figure 2.1**   The learning wave

gaining knowledge and developing ideas that encourage responses and so promote communication. Learning thus progresses from self-centred exploration towards social communication, and then with feedback progresses again; learning rolls on, the process is not always smooth, often like waves it may have its undertow when the preconceptions of old learning hold back the acceptance of new ideas.

The general process I have described is a commonsense description that may be applied to many aspects of early learning. It involves sensory exploration, sharing what you know with others, comparing their responses and reintegrating new ideas into your understanding – processes described by Piaget as Assimilation and Accommodation. It pertains to mathematical development when the child's sensory exploration relates to space and time and when it incorporates the use of the number module working with the physical senses to relate to quantities. The interrelations of personal and social activities are depicted in Figure 2.2.

A model like this might suggest to us that our teaching for children at very early stages of development should begin with a focus on personal exploration, using their senses to begin to appreciate and order the world about them – which we might describe as **personal maths**. As children develop, their own observations encourage them to communicate with others, to share, request and question. We might describe the processes that occur during communication, which relate to understanding and describing quantities, space, time and change, as **social maths**. Once the children have begun to grasp ideas, which constitute the personal and social background to

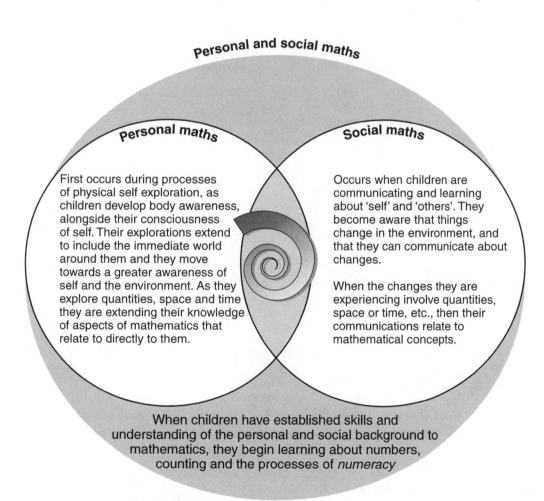

**Figure 2.2** Personal and social mathematics

5

maths, they begin to realise how to communicate, using those ideas for social and practical purposes. It is then that they are ready to appreciate and learn the beginning skills of **numeracy**. They do this by extending the innate skills of their number module; first learning to name the small quantities, and describe the order of relationships that previously they have only been able to 'sense'. Once they have begun, given the development of requisite physical and communication skills, they may move towards the ability to itemise groups, name quantities and numbers, then to count and describe numeric events.

This sequence of learning offers us a structure with which to enhance the early stages of the National Curriculum. Through it we can look in detail to describe activities that encourage biological, cognitive and social experiences that promote the bedrock mathematical understanding. A wealth of 'personal maths' occurs in sensory sessions, and 'social maths' occurs while communication is being promoted. In the past, mathematical detail within such experiences has not been part of our school curriculum. However, new guidance from the Qualifications and Curriculum Authority, intended to promote access to the National Curriculum for pupils at early stages of development, now recognises the importance of such dimensions of learning.

# 3 The strands of early mathematical learning

It is helpful for us to have an awareness of the natural course of learning, to provide guidance that helps us plan teaching strategies for children who have difficulties that disrupt normal patterns. There are similarities in the skills and processes that children use for gathering and understanding information in different areas of their development, or subjects. Though they are not uniquely 'mathematical', they do play roles in helping mathematical abilities evolve. So, through the course of this chapter, we will look at some common strands of early learning and how they intertwine and support mathematical learning.

## Introducing the tools and processes and content of early learning

There are a number of strands that are important; they represent physical and mental tools that children use to learn with, and processes in which they use the tools and through which they learn. Each of the strands is composed of a number of threads; none work in isolation. To understand how learning happens it helps if we unravel the braid.

### Tools for early learning

One important strand might be described as tools for learning. The tools are skills that develop from the sensory abilities that we are born with. The effectiveness with which we use them may be refined by usage and exercising them is itself part of the process of development. There are a number of threads within this strand, each thread representing a different type of tool. They are:

- sensation, attention and perception;
- sensory motor development;
- communication skills;
- concept development and thinking skills.

The tools of sensation, attention and perception work together to gather information for us. We use that information in our physical activities and manipulations: as we communicate with each other; and as we develop our thinking skills, ideas and concepts. On the journey of learning, all these mental activities associated with thinking, knowing and remembering, must work together. Collectively they are known as cognitive processes, and in practice their work is intertwined and inseparable. Throughout this book we will at times try to unravel them, in order to understand their functions. In so doing we must always remember that we are simplifying the processes. In the practical reality of learning they have complex relations by virtue of working together – the strength of the rope is more than the sum of its threads.

Skills deriving from these tools are used to collect and process information. There are obvious barriers that make it difficult for children with physical, sensory or cognitive impairments to develop them. If children lack any of the skills it is clear that we need to help them develop, or find, alternative compensatory skills. However, that is not to advocate for a curriculum that devotes itself only to teaching 'skills'. We must remember that in the natural course of learning children do not develop skills in isolation; learning progresses as they use existing skills to participate in activities and exploration. Feeling an inherent reward from an activity or the content of learning is an intrinsic stimulus that motivates the cycle of development, it generates the desire to repeat, rehearse, practise and advance. This cycle is demonstrated powerfully when children are engrossed in learning and willing to practise almost obsessively. Much of children's play is actually rehearsal of kinaesthetic learning exampled in the way that the young dancer portrayed in the film *Billy Elliot* incorporates dance steps into his way of walking home from school, which takes us to the next strand.

### Processes that use the skills of early learning

The activities that children participate in are the second strand of learning. They are processes that use the skills, and they give life, interest and breadth to the curriculum by drawing in content from the real world and encouraging the positive activity of exploration. Such processes both stimulate and use learning. Threads in this strand are (SCAA 1996):

- *Investigation* – stimulus response; exploration; discriminating; associating, connecting and chaining; concept learning.
- *Problem solving* – combining concepts, using them together; realising rules; anticipating results.
- *Interpretation* – using rules, applying them to other situations; transferring learning. Generalising connecting/creating new combinations.

These processes are the means by which children come to recognise and understand, they are the everyday face of what psychologists describe as 'cognitive processes'. As children use these processes they gather experience, and generate further opportunities and desire to experience and act upon the environment. The effective development of a child's physical and sensory learning tools and the processes of cognition exploration are intertwined. It will be evident to any of us who watch the remarkable process of young children exploring their world that at the very same time as young children *learn to use* their sensory, physical and mental tools, they *learn by using* their tools; learning to use the tools of learning is learning to learn.

The majority of children have made such great strides in the development of their cognitive abilities before they start school that teachers take many cognitive skills for granted, and they are not an explicit part of the curriculum. Children with very special needs however, are delayed in their learning and may need to be helped in the processes that other children naturally develop. Later in the book we will look at how the course and processes of cognitive development progress, and how such learning is an important part of learning about mathematics.

Content of the learning experience

The third strand of early learning is the content. When the 'skills and processes' are brought to bear on subject content they promote the development of related concepts and abilities; the relationship is illustrated in Figure 3.1. In the case of maths the content is about quantities, shapes, space and time. Learning it and applying it is a two-way street.

Quoted in the National Curriculum 2000, Professor Ruth Lawrence of the University of Michigan describes maths as the 'Study of patterns abstracted from the world around us' and she says, 'so anything we learn in maths has literally thousands of applications in arts, sciences, finance, health and leisure'. We have seen in Chapter 1 that mathematics has a particular flavour of content. At its fundamental levels it is essential to everyday life and social development. Children need to learn to assimilate and communicate information about quantities, time and space. They need to appreciate comparisons and differences, anticipate changes, in order to understand, and have some control of the world around them and make decisions

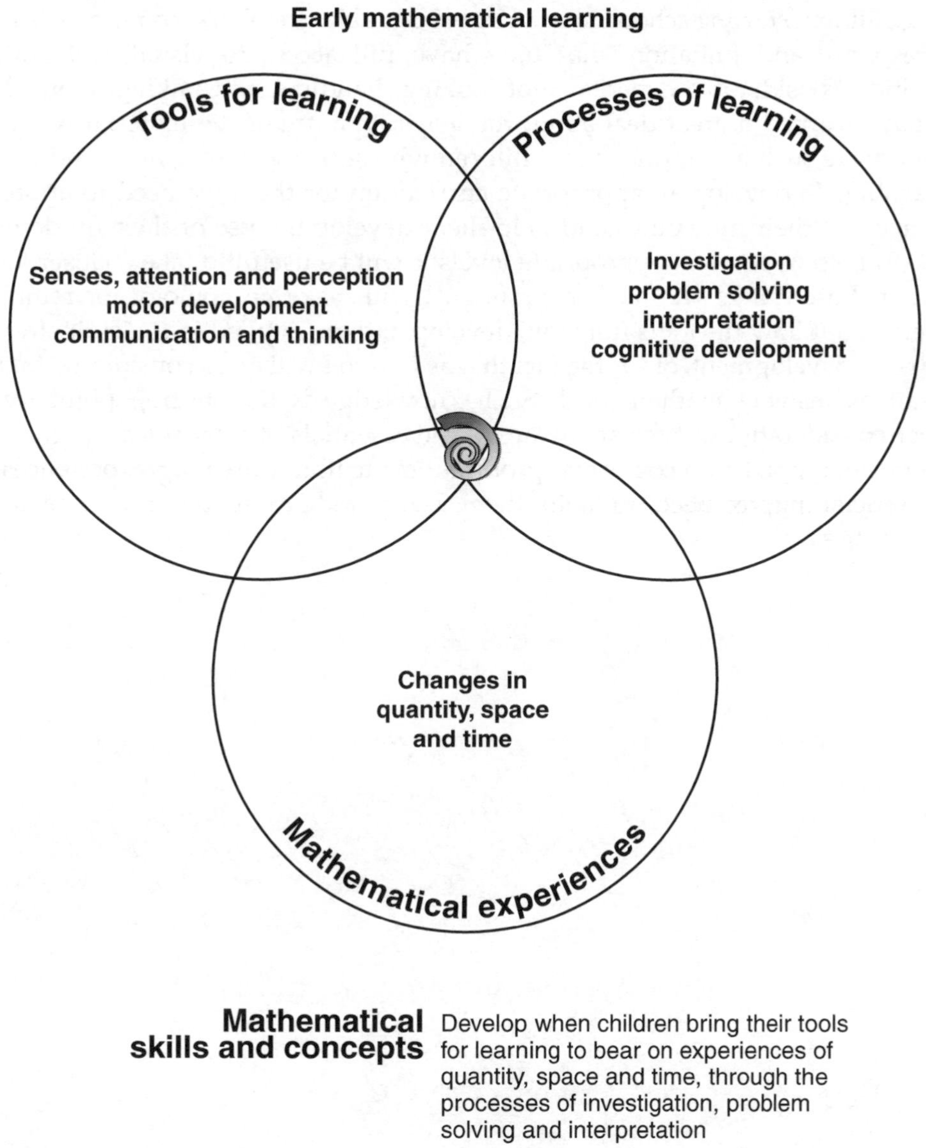

**Early mathematical learning**

**Tools for learning**

Senses, attention and perception
motor development
communication and thinking

**Processes of learning**

Investigation
problem solving
interpretation
cognitive development

Changes in
quantity, space
and time

**Mathematical experiences**

**Mathematical skills and concepts** Develop when children bring their tools for learning to bear on experiences of quantity, space and time, through the processes of investigation, problem solving and interpretation

**Figure 3.1**   The strands of early mathematical learning

and communicate about their lives. So grasping and using fundamental mathematical ideas, integrating them into their practical lives and wider communication skills is a vital facet of their needs. In later chapters we will explore how the strands of the National Numeracy Strategy relate to such fundamental mathematics.

## Why we need a close look in the tool box

Young children progress so rapidly with their learning that even when we have a sense of wonder about it, we still take much for granted. Most of us walk and perceive and judge the space around us so easily, identify quantities we need so readily, interpret numbers so rapidly, that we find it difficult to understand the effects of sensory deficits, cognitive or communication difficulties that make learning difficult for pupils with special needs. We take the tools of learning for granted. It is evident that this is true in the mainstream of mathematics teaching because the Numeracy Strategy teaching programmes from Reception onwards assume that young children starting school have already been able to embark upon early learning via response and imitation; that they have full access to visual and auditory memories, considerable experience of looking, handling and talking about things and have learned a great deal about the general nature of the material world. We cannot make such assumptions for children who suffer severe or profound barriers to learning. To develop an appropriate curriculum for them we need to appreciate the effects of their difficulties and help them develop the use of their fundamental tools. To help us focus at appropriate levels it will be useful to take a closer look at some of those things we take for granted. I will make no apology for reminding readers about how the tools function, develop and are applied in the mainstream of children's development, or for the fact that as I do so I will often consider factors that are not exclusively mathematical. Such knowledge is the starting point for our deeper considerations; if we are aware of the essentials of typical learning, we will be better equipped to recognise appropriate content and learning experiences that very special pupils need to help them learn and apply the fundamentals of mathematics.

# Part Two
# The tools of learning

## 4 | Tools working together

### Making sense of the world

As an individual we stand in a world that pulsates with energy. Within us is the silent darkness of the brain; how does the world get in there, what is it we see? There are three sets of tools, illustrated in Figure 4.1, that work together to help us make sense of our world.

- **Senses** – through stimulation of receptors by our sense organs we detect physical energy directly from the external or internal environment; we encode that energy into neural signals.
- **Perception** – processes by which the brain organises and interprets sensory information.
- **Attention** – through selective attention we choose what we need or want to take notice of, homing in on stimuli that may be important and cutting out the interference of background effects; it is the root of both our restlessness and our concentration.

Through the interaction of these processes we make our representation of the world, as we see, hear, touch, feel, or smell it. We create our own conscious experience. These wonders of neurochemistry are so fantastic that the Technicolor movie of our life usually seems to happen instantaneously; unlike on this Pentium computer, we do not have to wait for our web page of life to download; we can process colours, quantities, sounds, smells and feelings instantly, quickly turning them into feelings and meanings – we can even change our minds as rapidly. In everyday experience, Sensation, Perception and Attention blend; to understand their interaction we need to slow them down and reveal their parts.

### Sensation

The process of sensation is the entry level for learning information, and our sensory detectors are potentially very sensitive. The absolute thresholds of what we can discern are remarkable. Standing on the top of a mountain on an utterly clear, still night, given normal senses we can see the flame of a candle on another mountain 30 miles away. In a silent room we can hear a watch tick 20 feet away, we can feel the wing of a bee upon our cheek. We can smell a single drop of perfume in a three-room apartment (Galanter 1962).

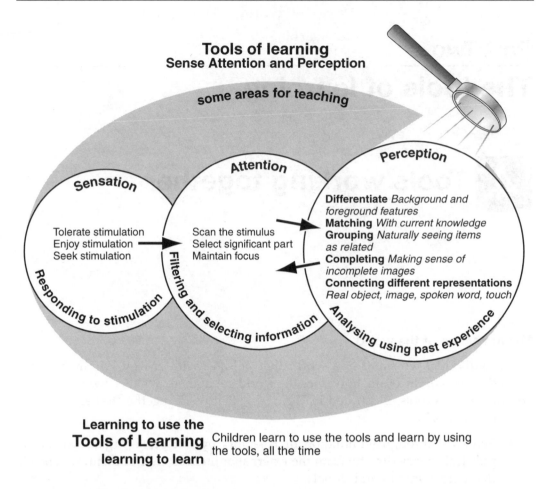

**Figure 4.1** The tools of learning

An important skill of sensation is to have the ability to detect important small differences in stimuli when we need to and yet be able to disregard even large but unimportant stimuli – that is, put stimuli into useful perspective, like a violinist in the street would hear his notes precisely but would be oblivious of a bus passing, so that the actual thresholds we use vary. Our ability to detect sensory signals depends not only on strength of signal but also on our psychological state, experience, expectations and fatigue, or heightened response due to context. When different senses are working well together they provide context that helps us to put signals in perspective; for example, if we see someone go through a door that slams we may be a little annoyed, but a visually impaired child will have had no warning and would be startled, and not knowing what had happened might be afraid of imminent danger. Sensory impairments and neural shortcomings can lead to difficulties in recognising and coordinating levels of stimulation.

## Perception

We might envisage our sense receptors feeding information up to the higher perceptual level processes, where we interpret what the senses detected. But perception is a process of construction and it not only draws on the information coming up from sensation, but it also uses our expectations, drawing down past experience from memory to make intelligent guesses about what we are looking at. There are many examples of perceptual illusion where we see particular content in drawings because some expectation or contextual effect creates a perceptual set that prompts our interpretation. Our belief influences what we see – it might be said we see what we believe (Shepard 1990). If this is true for our agile and well practised brains, then the process of building a perceptual representation of the world must be full of considerable pitfalls for children with sensory difficulties, who do not have the same fund of sensory memories to draw from.

## Attention

At the same time as our senses are feeding our perceptions, the processes of attention are making sure that we are not overloaded, by filtering out sensations that are of secondary importance, such as the feeling of the watch strapped to your wrist. Nobody needs to be continually reminded that his or her shoes are on for sixteen hours in a day. Sensations outside the focus of what you are immediately interested in will only be selected and rise to the surface of your conscious thinking if something within them seems attractive or important enough to demand attention, for example when background noise suddenly contains your name, or there is the smell of chocolate, or a tickle like a spider on your ankle. Then you are distracted or refocused, depending on how you see it. This description seems to suggest that attention is a process of excluding unnecessary demands, but the selectiveness also works by predisposing us to notice changes, through a process of sensory adaptation. For example, when we enter a room and are struck by a slightly unpleasant smell, we are gradually able to reduce our attention to it. Though sensory adaptation reduces our sensitivity, it provides an important benefit in that it offers us the opportunity to focus on informative changes, our attention is alert to novelty – if we bore our senses with constant stimulation or repetition, they will seek new information. Even a visual image will decay and move us on to seek new stimulus, although this effect is not noticeable to us normally because we constantly refresh our vision by flickering and scanning. This reinforces an important lesson – we perceive the world not exactly as it is, but as it is useful to us.

## When there are difficulties with the tools

When any of the tools of learning, sensation, perception and attention, are damaged or when children have difficulty in using them together then they have difficulty learning.

Failures of perception may occur anywhere between sensory detection and perceptual interpretation, and different circumstances will lead to different kinds of learning difficulties. For example, when a person is born with cataracts and unable to detect light, failure occurs because the visual processing parts of the brain do not receive stimulation, so nothing is registered. While children who have suffered damage to parts of the temporal lobe of the brain may have complete visual sensation, they may be unable to complete some perceptual processes; for example, they may be unable to recognise familiar faces, give meaning to symbols, or relate quantity value to groups. In both cases the children occupy the same world but will have very different perceptions of it. These children will need to make use of alternative sensory channels to gather information about shape, space and quantities. It is an immense challenge to teachers to begin to envisage the world of children who are affected by sensory difficulty or multisensory difficulties, and find compensatory strategies to help them make useful perceptual constructions. It may be an even greater challenge to envisage the effects of neural difficulties, which might even be undiagnosed. To help us meet those challenges it will be useful to consider in greater detail the features of sensation, perception and attention, and ways that they contribute to fundamental learning and mathematical experiences.

# 5 Sensation – the entry level of mathematics

**Modes of sensory experience**

New curriculum guidelines published in 2001, that are intended to describe access to the National Curriculum for pupils with learning difficulties, emphasise that staff can make mathematics more accessible by focusing on the senses.

In the examples I chose to use when introducing how senses, perception and attention work together I quoted instances that affected visual perception, but we receive information from seven sensory modes and the different ways in which we receive information has different implications for how we can use it and how we can retain it, and so affects the ways in which it contributes to our learning. Three of the sensory modes enable us to receive information from a distance.

Distance modes

- **Visual** – Light is interpreted through photo receptors of the eye and transmitted to regions of brain that decode visual information.
- **Auditory** – Rhythmic changes in air pressure, sound is transmitted physically through the ear and changed to neural impulses by tiny hairs in the inner ear and passed to the brain.
- **Olfactory** – Chemicals carried on air are detected by hair cells in our nose, producing electrical impulses transmitted to the olfactory cortex of brain. Being the first of distance senses to evolve, it has a powerful influence on non-cerebral functions such as moods, emotions and motivational states.

Two other modes inform us through direct contact.

Immediate modes

- **Tactile** – Information arrives via direct contact with skin in three forms: pressure, temperature and pain. Special receptors for each of these are located in various levels of the skin and pass information to a somatosensory area of cerebral cortex. (But pain has links direct to the spinal cord in a neural reflex that results in rapid muscle action.)
- **Gustatory** – Taste is the chemical detection of molecules dissolved in saliva. Taste and smell interact – taste plus smell equals flavour; and as with smell, taste creates powerful reactions.

In addition to the five familiar senses, we receive information from sixth and seventh less well recognised but vitally important modes, which use internal receptors, we might think of them as the eyes of the body.

Internal modes

- **Kinaesthetic sense** – In general terms relates information about internal states of the body. But an important special aspect is also information about body movement, transmitted to the brain by receptors known as proprioceptors in the skeletal system and joints, muscles and tendons which give us a sense of position.
- **Vestibulatory sense** – Sensors in the inner ear also provide a companion to kinaesthetic sense, sometimes described as an equilibrium or gravity sense that provides information about balance and motion.

## When there are sensory difficulties

In the normal course of events it is reasonable to agree with the statement (QCA 1999) that 95 per cent of what we learn comes through what we hear and see, because these distance senses reach out and collect so much information at our conscious level we regard them as primary. When children suffer from multisensory impairment, caused by damage to sense organs, or by neural difficulties that prevent them effectively attending to and drawing meaning from sensory information, then it becomes very important to seek not only how to make best use of what they have but also find ways of accessing some compensatory experience using other senses.

### The learning environment for sensory impaired children

Obviously the environment in which children are learning needs to be organised to help them access experiences, appreciate and explore resources, or space and events. It needs to ensure that they are stimulated and not confused. This includes providing optimal lighting that minimises glare, and making good use of contrast to help important stimuli stand out; reducing background noise, reverberation and auditory clutter to minimise confusion, and keeping the hearing environment as clear as possible.

### Compensating for the loss of incidental learning

To flag up ways in which fundamental mathematical learning is affected it is worthwhile for us to consider some ways in which general learning is affected when there are sensory difficulties. We should be aware that children usually have a vast experience of common objects – chairs, cups, plates, doors, stairs – the list is endless, simply from having seen them around all their lives. Their mobility also means that the opportunity to extend their visual experience through touch and movement is simply there for the taking, learning is easily within their grasp. Because vision can give information about events happening at a distance children are usually able to learn a great deal from imitating other people. They observe groups of objects and see what quantities are and see them change. They are able to visualise the effects of changes, able to see what space is and judge movement, direction and speed against visual referents. The visually impaired child on the other hand is deprived of much of this contextual information about the things in their world, and their experience of judging changes is constrained. Most of us use visual memories of the room, or space, we are in and the things in it. We can continually keep track on how things are changing, and if we need to remind ourselves about some feature, like how many cups are on the table, we can look back and refresh. Some of those visual memories recur so often that we are able to construct generalised visualisations, like three cups, that stay with us and become tools of our memory and thinking, concepts of form, space and quantity. We will see later how important this is in developing understandings of number and processes of numeracy. For pupils who are blind the room is a series of touch and movement experiences, and so the memory of space or movable objects is difficult to refresh. We would normally supplement our visual information with clues from sound and memories of touch and movement; instead of being an integrated set, these become primary for the visually impaired child. Of course problems are compounded for children who have additional hearing difficulties, or children with mobility difficulties who are constrained in their search for kinaesthetic and tactile clues.

Related problems will also occur for children who may have full use of their sensory receptors and physical abilities, but suffer neural difficulties that generate autistic behaviours that hinder them in the processes of recognising and connecting the significance of some features of stimulus. Such children may also be tactile and auditory defensive. They may remain unaware, or be over aware of stimulus, and thus unable to effectively integrate information that would normally generate constructive curiosity, be explored and become part of experience and knowledge. These aspects will reoccur when we consider the effects of attention difficulties.

*Compensatory stimulation and tactile defensiveness*
It is well appreciated that many people who suffer blindness develop more acute hearing skills; for example, using sound and echo to enhance their sense of location and space. We cannot, however, assume that children automatically develop sharpened compensatory senses, and we must adopt teaching strategies to help develop them. Having said that we must also remember that sensory deprivation leaves children vulnerable and unexpected stimulation can be startling or even frightening when they do not know what is happening. They may generalise these responses, becoming defensive against new experiences, and even developing strategies to avoid stimulation. There will be further discussion of such complex barriers to learning in the section about attention. To help avoid startling and generating defensive reactions we would be wise to adopt sensitive approaches to giving children things, and offer them the opportunity to anticipate the taking experience, tickle their curiosity – using a vocal lead in and perhaps first touching some less sensitive part of their body, perhaps the shoulder, with the object before bringing it into the proximity of their grasp; by sliding it down their arm to the back of their hand which they may then naturally turn to take the object, with a feeling of being in control.

In the face of sensory defensiveness, a first and ongoing teaching brief is to ensure that children learn to tolerate, enjoy and seek stimulation; the development of confident curiosity, and feeling control of your environment, is a vital element of this. Though this learning is about the child's personal development and seems so fundamental that one would normally expect it to be established during the early days and months of life, it is still a necessary aspect of learning to work towards mathematical concepts, for example as children learn to anticipate or communicate about magnitude, duration, and frequency of interesting, pleasant, or unpleasant stimulus.

*The sensory content of the fundamental mathematics curriculum*
When sensory difficulties have limited a child's opportunities to collect a fund of incidental learning, which is composed of memories in different sensory modes all working together, they will have restricted understanding of many concepts and aspects of language that we usually take for granted. For example, very young

infants usually learn about transferring objects from hand to hand – an early experience of one–two – and a foundation experience of sequence and pattern. Likewise they are deeply aware of how it feels to hold two objects, and how it will be different if another is added or dropped. They associate these and a myriad of tactile memories with word sounds they hear accompanying them; they develop a fund of such background data to compare with and integrate into new experiences. All this is achieved using senses together; when a link in the chain is broken those connections, internal images and relationships may be incomplete.

Yet it is still all too easy for us to assume that all children have similar appreciations to ourselves and relate them to the words about quantity and change that we use when we talk to them. Connecting tactile and kinaesthetic experience with language is vitally important. We must communicate through our touch, body language and vocalisation to support experiences that trigger sensations of change and sequence, and accompany such sensation with associated language. But not just verbally, because intonation and rhythm carry much important information, creating anticipation, raising questions, confirming answers, expressing size, equality, and very importantly intonation and rhythm are keys to motivating learners to attend and respond.

In providing experiences we need to recognise the power of kinaesthetic and tactile signals, incorporating and modelling movement, reach and touching into learning activities. Though the distance senses of vision and hearing are credited with an enormous proportion of our learning potential, we would be unable to function without our kinaesthetic sense, unable to stand in balance and move, unable to feed ourselves. I do not need vision to put chocolate in my mouth; Evelyn Glennie, the percussionist, plays music with the world's greatest orchestras without the benefit of hearing, and she probably closes her eyes when the experience of playing *The Flight of the Bumblebee* is at its height. The direct and internal senses providing us with tactile and kinaesthetic information are much underestimated.

They make enormous contributions to our every function, through memory of touch, motion and vibration; they are also senses that have very direct relation with form, weight, space. The pressure and muscular tension created by grasping and holding objects will inform our developing understanding of mass, because the function of proprioceptors would be providing us with information about size and weight as we reached out our arms and drew them together preparing to grasp objects. All these ideas point to important roles for tactile and kinaesthetic activities as alternative and supplementary modes of learning about form, mass, space and quantity. Indeed perhaps they are equally important, but underestimated or neglected modes, because we are not usually very conscious of their function.

Thinking about the role of proprioceptors in developing our understanding of form, space and weight reminds me of Einstein's description about how his mathematical thinking initially involved what he called 'some kind of physical feeling'. I am attracted to the idea that the fundamental understandings that our special children need to develop about their world are pursued by similar processes to those the great genius used to deduce the relationship between energy and mass at the cosmic level.

So we need to ensure that our pupils are exposed to the power of tactile and kinaesthetic experience; that they experience sensations of pressure and motion and have them associated with language describing weight and space. They need experience reaching and holding and associate them with language of size, or feel rhythmic limb movements and associate them with vocabulary of sequence, frequency and number. Experience comparative weight on limbs and hands, sequential touching of hands, fingers and feet, shifting hands from one object to another, moving things, giving, taking and changing. Experience transfer of weight between feet, or with held objects. These are a multitude of experiences that we usually take for granted, but through which typical children have been busy experiencing and absorbing the fundamentals of mathematics long before they start school. They are the parts of mathematics that the National Curriculum before 2001 failed to reach, but we can include them within the strands of the Numeracy Strategy because they include experiences of quantities and changes of size, they relate to shape, weight and movement and include the processes of facing problems and making things change.

# 6 Perception – making sense of sensations

Perception is a complex process, filtering, attending to and interpreting sensory information in what seems an instant. Most children's perceptual skills are well developed before they reach school age, but problems spawn learning difficulties. It is important for us to consider how we can include developing perceptual skills within our fundamental maths curriculum. Some aspects of perception that children need to master include:

- **Differentiating features** within a stimulus, e.g. visually separating background and foreground, or being able to select foreground sound, or relevant tactile stimuli.
- **Matching**, both in the sense of recognising similarity, and in respect of corresponding new stimuli to existing knowledge.
- **Completing**, being able to make sense of incomplete, images or events; this might include tactile or kinaesthetic memories of objects, quantities in groups, spaces, etc.
- **Connecting** representations to meaning, including connecting pictures or symbols to real objects, spoken words to meaning.

All of these activities are part of the general processes of learning, but when they deal with recognising quantities, numerals, shapes, etc., then they are part of learning mathematics. Hiding and revealing all or parts of items and groups, collecting matched items, can be the basis or component parts of games, or can be made the focus of everyday events that are organised to provide motivated learning opportunities.

## Organising perception

If we look at how perception is normally organised we might see ways that its component skills can be promoted. It seems our mind has inborn tendencies to organise fragmentary sensory information into whole perceptions and there are several ways that it does this. They were originally described by a group of German psychologists, who described them as Gestalt principles, gestalt meaning 'Whole'. The gestalt principles are clear examples of the interpretive powers of the mind. They show how raw sensations begin to take on meaning through associations that we make. Examples given usually relate to visual perception, but the principles do come into play in other senses, and envisaging how to extend the principles within other sensory domains is important to us in finding avenues of communication and learning for children with multisensory impairments.

## Perception of form

There are a number of areas that work together to enable us to perceive the form of objects. They are important to the growth of understanding about objects, space, shape. In addition, they offer many points for us to consider about how we present experiences and teaching materials to children.

### *Figure and ground*

The first task of perception is to distinguish any figure or object from its background. As we read, printed words are the figure of our attention. The paper, including any pictures over which words are printed, must remain in the background of our consciousness as we scan if we are to discern the words. Figure 6.1 is an example not only of how our mind seeks to make meaning from the areas of light and dark but also of how the same stimulus can trigger more than one perception; it can be seen in two different ways but not at the same time. With sound we select certain voices to listen to and do not attend much to the hubbub, though we use our vision along with our hearing to help us locate speakers and make decisions about what to listen to. This support is not available as a filtering tool for visually impaired people, and may be restricted for children with attention difficulties or profound limitations to movement. In addition, without the aid of visual reference to locate and cross-check the source of stimulus, it is difficult to discern the boundaries of space or shape, e.g. workspace, locate sound, or establish the tactile, spatial or auditory background and foreground within which we need to focus for judgements of quantity, shape, etc.

### *Grouping*

Having discriminated important features from the background it is necessary to organise the features into meaningful form. Basic sensations of movement, colour, contrast of light and dark are processed immediately, but then we seem to follow certain rules for grouping the information. There are several principles of grouping that come into play in this process, Proximity, Similarity, Continuity, Closure, and Combination or Connectedness. (They are described in Figure 6.2.) The principles are not equal – for example, proximity will override similarity, closure will override proximity – but together they add up to a powerful tendency to perceive visual information in terms of figures against backgrounds. When we encounter sensory experience, in order to make sense of it some feature leaps forward as important. We see objects as items, not random patterns, of light; we visually collect the items into groups or patterns that we can remember visually, which helps us relate to our existing visual memories. Similarly, we normally pick out specific sounds and sound patterns, rather than experience a confusing wall of sound. After feeling the form of a whole object with the whole of our hands we usually seek the detail

**Perceiving the foreground.**
Do you see two faces or a vase? We can see one or the other but not both at the same time.

**Figure 6.1**   Figure and background image

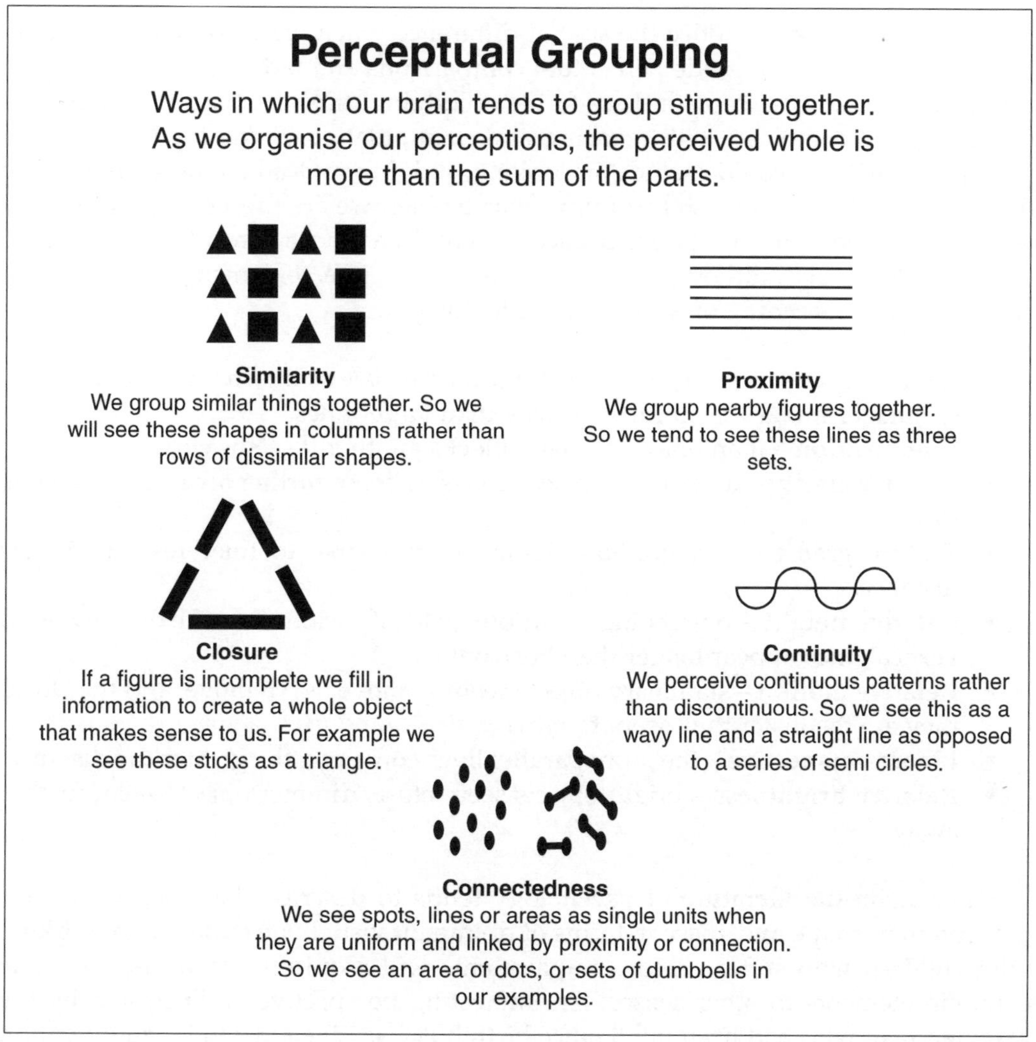

## Perceptual Grouping

Ways in which our brain tends to group stimuli together.
As we organise our perceptions, the perceived whole is
more than the sum of the parts.

**Similarity**
We group similar things together. So we
will see these shapes in columns rather than
rows of dissimilar shapes.

**Proximity**
We group nearby figures together.
So we tend to see these lines as three
sets.

**Closure**
If a figure is incomplete we fill in
information to create a whole object
that makes sense to us. For example we
see these sticks as a triangle.

**Continuity**
We perceive continuous patterns rather
than discontinuous. So we see this as a
wavy line and a straight line as opposed
to a series of semi circles.

**Connectedness**
We see spots, lines or areas as single units when
they are uniform and linked by proximity or connection.
So we see an area of dots, or sets of dumbbells in
our examples.

**Figure 6.2**   Gestalt principles for perceptual grouping of sensory stimuli

of an object with our fingertips, and thus build a tactile map. As mentioned earlier, vision usually plays an important associative role in locating, confirming and remembering the boundaries of other sensory experiences, so when visual reference is disrupted, holding memories of tactile and spatial patterns and relations is particularly difficult. Though sound patterns are strongly recognised and remembered, their ephemeral nature presents memory difficulties because the stimulus cannot be refreshed.

*Depth perception*
Perception of depth is an important aspect not only of our ability to understand the space in which we move but also to appreciate size. Newborn animals and very young infants show an awareness of depth at a self-preservatory level, which has suggested that some depth perception is present at birth (Gibson and Walk 1960). To appreciate depth we need to transform the two-dimensional images upon our retinas into three-dimensional perceptions. An important way that we are able to make this transformation is by using binocular clues. This is when the brain compares the slightly different image from each eye, along with muscular clues about how much we are converging our eyeballs. Of course our perception presents us with a combined image and we are thus unaware of the binocular process of depth

judgement – unless we notice the spatial difference when we close one eye, we do use monocular clues to guide perceptual comparisons and judgements. Our special pupils may need practice with these facets of judging three-dimensional shape and space, usually combined with reaching and manipulation. Some aspects of depth perception that we could include in looking, judging and adjusting activities are listed below. They could also be of importance when we are presenting images and teaching materials, or sensory experiences, to children whose perceptual abilities are not fully developed, although they are capable of either enhancing or confusing children's understanding of what they are looking at.

- **Relative size** – our image of objects reduces in size as they are further from us, so smaller images seem further away than larger ones.
- **Interposition** – if an image partially blocks another it seems closer.
- **Relative clarity** – we perceive hazy objects as being further away, clear ones as close.
- **Texture gradient** – a gradual change from coarse to finer texture signals distance.
- **Relative height** – objects higher in our field of vision seem further away, so vertical lines appear longer than horizontals.
- **Relative motion** – stationary objects seem to move as we move, and the closer they are the faster they seem to move.
- **Linear perspective** – the more parallel lines converge, the greater the distance.
- **Relative brightness** – bright objects seem close, dimmer objects seem further away.

Once again the literature of psychology tends to describe these aspects of our perception of shape and space in terms of dominant visual perception, and working with children who suffer sensory impairments will require us to transpose some common elements to other senses. An interesting perspective is illustrated by the case of a man who had been blind since birth but was given vision by an operation (Gregory and Wallace 1963). He could recognise objects that he had touched while he was blind, e.g. objects in rooms and the window frame, but was unable to interpret the distant view from the window, because he had no tactile experience of such distances. In fact he thought he would be able to reach out and touch the ground. It is likely that he had concepts of rooms because he had tactile, kinaesthetic and vestibular memory maps, and from the generalisation of these memories he may have developed concepts relating to mobility in limited spaces. These concepts may be supported by other sensory information, like the resonance and echo that offer distance and quality clues for hearing, that are akin to visual size, clarity, brightness, and perspective clues.

## Perceptual constancy

All the above facets of depth perception are about relationships, how we perceive things depending upon their distance and position. Another element about perceptions of size, and distance, is understanding perceptual constancy. For example, if we watch a door open, the image we see changes from a rectangle, it becomes increasingly trapezoidal and eventually we see only the narrow strip of its edge. Or we see a car some distance down the road and it looks small, but we still know that when it arrives it will be big enough for us to get into.

We perceive familiar objects as having constant form even though the stimulus we receive from them changes. Thanks to this perceptual constancy we are usually able to recognise things instantly; without it we would be completely confused, constantly reworking out the new meaning of stimulus. Perceptual constancy highlights for us the close relationship between perceiving distance and size.

- Perceiving an object's distance away from us gives us a clue to its size.
- Having an idea about its general size helps us perceive its distance from us.

There is evidence about cultural differences affecting perceptions of distance. People who are used to living in modern buildings subconsciously use the angles of room corners to judge distances in rooms, and forest dwelling peoples find it difficult to accept that creatures seen as tiny in the far distance are not insects but buffalo (Turnbull 1961). Related evidence shows people from isolated cultures have difficulties interpreting photographs as three-dimensional representations, whereas in western cultures children frequently exposed to picture books readily accept images of objects as being 'the same'. Together these observations indicate that our experience and the environment we frequent have effect on how we will refine our skills. Native Australian children are commonly more able to draw upon smell as a source of information than white Australians (Dodd 1989); forest dwelling peoples have hearing finely tuned to locate direction and distance of sound. This reminds us of two things important for us in work with children who have learning or sensory difficulties.

Firstly, our taken for granted perceptions of the world actually depend upon our experience, and we cannot take for granted that children with learning difficulties have acquired appropriate levels of perceptual experience. Size and distance judgements, or associating pictures and symbols with objects, or recognising the equivalences of sizes and quantities, may not be easy for them. Experiences that help children develop their powers of recognition of shape, space, and quantity, at these fundamental perceptual levels, are appropriate content for the elemental maths curriculum.

Secondly, though vision is the dominant sense, alternatives can provide vital information for perceptions. It is essential that we promote the integrated use of senses, not only where children are visually impaired, but with all pupils. To this end we need to ensure that teaching strategies and learning activities include multisensory materials and experience, offering a variety of ways to access and respond to information in order to maximise the range of association between perceptual clues from all senses.

## Perceptual sets – prepare you for what you think is there

We appreciate the inference within the well-known saying, 'Seeing is believing', but maybe do not realise how much the other side of the coin is also true, that 'believing is seeing'. Our experiences and assumptions create an anticipatory framework, psychologists describe as a 'Perceptual Set'. The perceptual set inclines us to interpret stimuli into meanings that we expect. It may be this kind of activity that leads us to see the Loch Ness monster when a curved log is floating in the lake. There are a number of ways that predispose us to these ways of thinking; the most powerful is expectation. If you have just been looking at numbers you would be more likely to interpret ambiguous symbols as numbers rather than letters. (This is illustrated in Figure 6.3.) Our face recognition skills prime us to see faces, in caricatures, random configurations, and even in the shadows of the moon.

The examples above are all immediate perceptual effects, but there are some related longer-term effects, that connect to behaviour. For example, certain smells or sounds may prompt us to anticipate events and lead us to prepare ourselves for

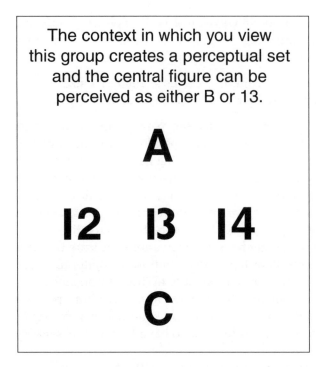

The context in which you view this group creates a perceptual set and the central figure can be perceived as either B or 13.

A

12   13   14

C

**Figure 6.3**   Perceptual sets

them; all of these effects could be important to consider when preparing children with sensory difficulties for learning experiences.

Perceptual sets can also be generated through motivational states; for example, people who are hungry may tend to associate ambiguous stimuli with food. Personal interests and values, and social prejudices have all been shown to prompt perceptual sets, and thus we might see that perceptual sets are powerful aspects of the obsessive interests that we often observe in people with attention disorders. So introducing positive sets, or minimising negative ones, may help children access learning.

*Perceptual sets and special children*

Objects of reference have come into common use in our schools for children with multisensory or communication difficulties, and they function not only as aids to communication but also as prompts to trigger appropriate perceptual sets, preparing children for activities. Actions and sounds or words might also be used to create sets of connections; for example, working with a child who has a visual impairment and physical difficulties, we might use words related to the exploration of size, shape or position while we assist or model reaching and feeling movements to help them develop a tactile 'image' and create associations, between sensations and words. Another effect could be that the child would associate those related words and movements with a certain kind of activity, and begin to realise that during this time they would be sharing and responding with another person to an exploration of the shape, size, and position of things in their environment; they would be conscious of taking part in an activity that had a specific flavour – mathematical experience.

For other examples, at later levels of learning, we might look at the early learning of counting; we may be inclined to think that when we hold out our palm revealing a group of Smarties and ask children, 'How many?', they are automatically transported to a perceptual set that brings number names that are associated with their concepts of quantity to mind. But maybe they do not associate the question with quantity; maybe they associate your actions with an offering. Or even if they do realise it is a question about quantity, they may connect rapidly to the 'temptation set', or the 'action – take it quick set'. We will see in later chapters that counting is a complex of skills and there are numerous sets of connections, at various levels, requiring appropriate perceptual sets, that we normally take for granted, but which with children who have delayed learning we may need to diagnose and develop.

I am reminded of the times in my past when I was face to face with Mandy, across a table on which might be a group of counters. My question 'How many' didn't prompt action, but it did prepare her to wait for me to prompt her by saying 'one', in a long encouraging tone. Whereupon she would point at the first object and say 'two' and proceed to count. She could never achieve accuracy because she always started on two, so we always ended up with a wrong feeling. The perceptual sets Mandy accessed when sitting opposite me were different to the ones I hoped she had, they were a ritual of misleading expectations. I needed to shift the perceptual set created in Mandy's mind by sitting facing each other, away from the ritual and on to the principles of counting (see Chapter 12).

### When there are shortcomings of perception

*Connecting and combining*

It is important to remember that perception is more than processing incoming sensory information; it also involves drawing down information from memories of past experience, comparing and matching them to the new sensory information, to help make intelligent guesses. We depend upon our previous knowledge to give us structures into which we fit new information and shape our perceptions. As Kant remarked, 'We see things not as they are, but as we are'. It is plain that shortcomings in existing ideas will confuse perceptions; this has obvious implications for children with sensory impairments. For example, the environment has less stimulus value for visually impaired children and they are restricted in their engagement within it. They may not recognise their impact on objects that they manipulate; do they have the same mental images of consequences as they rotate a cup of milk, as you do? They will not experience the same visual models, or have the same fund of visual memories to match against new stimuli (Hendrickson and McLinden 1977). For example, without a visual memory of teapots in use, it would be confusing to try to discriminate between the spout and the handle by touch. We will see later how early concepts of number develop through an interplay of visual imagery and touch. The development of good perceptual models usually requires an integrated use of the senses. When children have sensory difficulties, parts of those chains are missing and we need to help them make best use of what they have; making sure that they have lots of practical experience making complementary use of alternative strategies, and experience of recognising things from different view points, and anticipating the identity of partially obscured things, shapes or quantities. The evolution of the 'sensory curriculum' (Longhorn 1988) has provided many avenues for developing alternative channels. Innovative work has also conceived ways to organise environments that make stimulation accessible, e.g. Lilli Nielsen's (1987) little room and resonance boards, or Keith Park's (1997) use of tents. It is essential that these attitudes and techniques permeate the presentation of the mathematics curriculum for sensory impaired children, since one of their primary needs is to engage in exploration which helps them develop understanding of form, and changes as they affect their environment.

*Learning environments*

It is important to present sensory stimulation to pupils in ways that enable them to discriminate important features. They need to reduce confusion if they are to build useful perceptual models and make connections that form constructive perceptual sets. The practitioners mentioned above, Nielsen, Longhorn and Parks, all recognise the importance of providing environments in which children can focus on stimulus and participate in experiences that help them organise their perceptions. Their work, and the work of organisations such as the RNIB and SENSE, has led many schools to adopt quiet corners, low stimulus learning stations, effectively defined display techniques, etc.; and adopt teaching strategies that model and use multisensory exploration. The use of alternative avenues of communication such as signs, symbols or as mentioned earlier the use of objects of reference, has also become widespread as means that can prepare and orient children towards seeking appropriate stimulation and making sense of it.

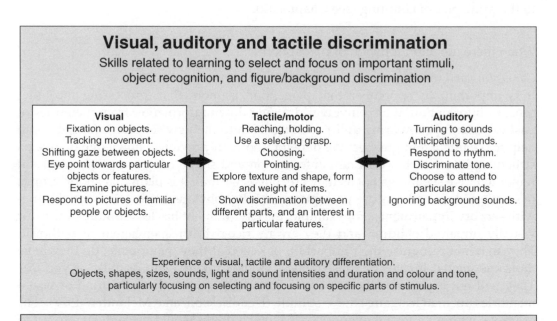

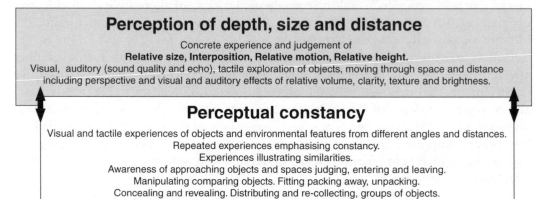

**Figure 6.4**  Teaching perceptual skills

*Curricular content*

In order to appreciate the experiences that will help them grasp the fundamentals of mathematical learning very special children need to learn to look with a purpose, they need to be prepared to search for meaning and remember what they have seen and be able to connect its meaning to new experiences. Discriminating between an object and its background, and beginning to expect a sense of constancy about that object, may seem very elementary skills, but with some very special pupils it is at this level that we begin to build the mathematical concept of One which is at the root of numeracy. All aspects of numeracy depend upon us having the powers of perception to gather information, about quantities, shape, space and time. So all of the aspects of form recognition, perceptual constancy and perceptual sets that we have surveyed above, and are reviewed in Figure 6.4, are appropriate parts of their mathematics curriculum. The activities that it describes can all be connected to events that involve children's exploration and experiences of quantity, shape, space and time. We can see from them that even approaching a door with a child in a wheelchair is a teaching opportunity as the door looms larger and we have to decide if we will fit through; taking the opportunity to emphasise all the sensory aspects of the event, and associate them with appropriate communication, is all contributing to understanding size, distance and motion; doing it repeatedly illustrates constancy, and so the understanding of our mathematical world unfolds. We could share a sense of awe with our children in an experience that illustrates similar concepts, by entering the turbine hall of the Tate Modern in London, experiencing its huge height and space, visually and through its sounds, touching and wondering at the huge sculptures it houses and then observing them from the successive floors as you travel up through the galleries using the stairs or lifts.

The ideas in Figure 6.4 offer some frameworks for teaching objectives that will reoccur in many combinations and at various levels in the practical activities we discuss later in the book. They have a part to play in activities that constitute an appropriate mathematics curriculum for pupils developing fundamental mathematical skills, which so importantly contribute to their practical lives and to their abilities to enjoy and use the form and patterns of the world around them.

# 7 Attention – choosing your material

## What is attention?

We take attention for granted, its work is integrated with the other tools of sense and perception, and it works on different levels. As teachers we become particularly agitated by inattention, but really there is no such thing, it is just that attention is looking elsewhere. To understand how to ensure our special children can use their powers of attention to look, or seek, where we want them to, it will benefit us to take a short tour of its deeper recesses.

There are limits to the amount of information we can attend to at any one time, and managing that workload requires adaptability. Through the processes of attention we choose what we need to take notice of, homing in on stimuli that may be important and cutting out the interference of background effects; it is the root of both our restlessness and our concentration. Early attempts by psychologists to describe how attention worked tended to look upon it rather mechanistically as a filtering system. But it is not just a passive system that receives and edits information; it is a very flexible process involving us in the active selection of what we attend to.

In previous chapters we have noted that sensation and perception would be chaos without some processes of selection prioritising what we pay attention to. At a party, we concentrate our attention towards the people talking within the close group, and seeming not to be paying attention to other conversations, because there would just be too much to listen to. Yet if someone in a nearby group mentions our name we are likely to become aware of their conversation, and scan it to see if we want to switch our attention to it. So although we filter out unwanted stimuli we do not block it all out completely, we keep scanning for signals of interest. This suggests that incoming information is processed at some level without our being aware of it. Another benefit of this is that we do not need to attend to the feel of our clothing unless it becomes uncomfortable.

A vast amount of our responses to stimuli result in seemingly automatic decisions and actions; we seem not to think about an action, we just do it. Neisser (1976) suggests that to achieve this rapid level of decision-making we use our store of past experience to cut down the need to recognise every stimulus as if it were new. He suggests that our processes form a continual cycle, anticipating what is likely to happen, scanning to see if these expectations are fulfilled, and then modifying them in the light of the information we receive. The expectations about what we are likely to perceive are known as anticipatory schema, they are sets of ideas we have about what is likely to happen based upon our past experience. During this processing we use all the strategies for making sense of sensation, which we described when discussing organising perception in Chapter 6. So we are actively, but unconsciously, scanning to discern figure and background, to group features together and make meaningful patterns, we are using our knowledge of all the aspects of depth perception and perceptual constancy to check new sensory information against our existing sets of perceptual understanding. If everything is as expected we can use the information automatically, and thus we are able to carry out many actions as routines seemingly without thought, indeed we have a tendency to plough that furrow on automatic pilot, a routine sequence of familiar stimulation and events. For example, how many of us have driven to work and suddenly realised we cannot remember anything about the journey, a frightening thought that seems to imply we were driving in a daze. In fact, during that journey, there are a lot of automatic processes all taking place simultaneously, and at different levels of importance – our breathing, sitting comfortably, the mechanical operation of car such as gear changes, driver observations, route finding, emergency awareness – all capable of shifting from the automatic pilot level, up into direct awareness, to focus conscious attention, and inspire action if needs be. During the process of scanning the world we tend to take in what we expect and go with the flow that we are used to. We are, however, continually open to new events, and sometimes they register very quickly to alert us, demanding evaluation, like a sudden movement in our peripheral vision, or flash of light. Sometimes they occur more gently, drawing our attention to a conscious level because features of the stimulus are not congruent with our existing knowledge, something like a blue banana would tickle our curiosity, or noticing a spelling mistake would momentarily halt the flow of overall comprehension as we read.

During the processes of attention we integrate the signals from all of our senses, and we prioritise between them. When we are very interested we do not notice the discomfort of our chair, when the film is boring we start taking in the tactile signals of discomfort and start to shuffle in our seats. Operating at different levels enables us to do more than one thing at a time, for example read this book and drink coffee, and as the mental demands of tasks change, we can change the share of attention we give to it. If, like many children with special needs, we have difficulties regulating or prioritising the stimulus we have to deal with at any time, our learning is seriously affected, and the quality of our lives. It will make it difficult for us to focus and connect salient features of our experiences.

## External factors affecting attention

The descriptions of attention that we have so far considered have been related to sensory and psychological procedures that feed our perceptual processes. There is however another, more commonly used, interpretation that reflects yet another level of application; it relates to our ability to apply and maintain concentration on tasks. While this everyday idea of attention seems to be about observable, practical things like paying attention in class, and paying attention to teaching materials, it shares many features of the theories we have been outlining.

There are a number of practical factors that relate to either the stimulus or the observer that influence attention. They are pertinent for all learners, but we should especially bear them in mind when we organise learning activities for pupils who may have sensory and attention difficulties. Some factors are external, and others are internal to the learner.

## Practical factors influencing attention

- **Intensity** – Loud noise, bright colours, strong odours, and high pressure on skin are all compelling stimuli. We need to consider these aspects not only in respect of using them judiciously to gain attention, but also when considering their effects on pupils who have difficulty controlling their attention and who may suffer over-stimulation.

- **Novelty** – New features of stimulus or unusual events attract attention. Novelty within stimulus maintains interest, but vice versa inappropriate new stimulus may distract, and continual presentation of new stimuli overloads us and generates anxiety or over-excitement.

- **Variation** – Stimulus needs to vary to keep our attention, otherwise as with a ticking clock we adapt to it. Teachers need to modulate the tone of their voice to keep children listening, use intonation to highlight the important parts of what they say; visual stimulation or teaching aids need to be changed to maintain interest.

- **Regularity** – The regularity of stimulus in time and space has an effect; distributed stimulus will attract because we become adapted to frequent, regular signals.

- **Colour** – Bright colours and contrasts are highlighted for attention, and while this is a commonly used feature, we should also realise that confusion of competing colour can make discrimination difficult, especially for the visually impaired, or be over-stimulating for pupils with attention difficulties.

- **High sounds** – Tend to attract, and should be used within the variation of stimuli as an aid to cues and prompts.

- **Conditioning** – Accustomed and habituated stimuli are likely to be picked out, for example your own name, a familiar tune, smell or well-loved image. Responses can be anchored to particular stimuli.

- **Cueing** – Vocal, verbal or pointing clues can prepare or draw attention to particular stimulus for learners. This is apparent in phrases like 'watch this', but another important means of cueing is found in the use of rising vocal intonation that highlights anticipation before an event, or punctuates the sequence, emphasising the importance of number names in a counting sequence. Both physical and eye pointing are important aspects of developing one to one appreciation, as well as the important counting skill of itemisation.

- **Touch** – When touching someone to draw their attention it is worth remembering that the surface sensors that experience light touch tend to be cued to raise alerting signals, while deep sensors have more inhibitory functions. Unexpected light touch can trigger alarm responses that may disrupt the inclination to learn, particularly fleeting touch from outside the field of vision, though well anticipated firm or enfolding touch can be calming.

- **Personal space** – Usually working in close proximity heightens awareness to sharing attention but many children with attention difficulties are very sensitive about their personal space and have problems when people are in close proximity.

Using attention strategies when teaching fundamental maths

The external factors that affect attention provide pointers for organising learning experiences and materials in ways that will help obtain and maintain attention. All teachers of all children, in all subjects, should be aware of attention functions at different levels of conscious and subconscious action. They should be adept at using characteristics such as intensity, variety, novelty, effective distribution of stimulus; they should take account of conditioning and developing effective techniques of cueing. Utilising a knowledge of these features will help to ensure that teaching has the power to take children through appropriate levels of attention, maintain good pace and make sure teaching materials have attention grabbing power.

Using strategies to make certain that our pupils are attracted to attend to the stimuli we want them to absorb is especially important when children suffer from barriers to learning. They provide valuable support at all stages of our maths teaching, from the earliest levels of experiential encounters through to the later levels where pupils are beginning to master numerical relations and processing. Facets of the strategies will affect our choices of resources and the way we organise and present activities. For example, if we are to work with a visually impaired child learning to count, we will immediately recognise the value of using two or three fluorescent yellow tennis balls on a deep blue tray that we were able to purchase from a market stall, as opposed to a set of plastic counters. Not only do the balls have good contrast with the tray, which will help make best use of any vision that the child does have, but they have attractive tactile qualities. The balls are good to grasp, they create a much stronger tactile signal when one ball is held in each hand than a counter in each palm would. They are large enough to induce large movements when handling them, so picking up and passing them in turn to another person will create kinaesthetic sensations that relate to turn sequence and frequency, which can be connected by the teacher to quantity words like another or more, or to number words. Extending even further, the balls make a good sound when they are dropped into a biscuit tin, and so yet another sensory dimension offers us opportunity to develop the attention grabbing and maintaining powers of these simple yet effective resources. A little knowledge about the facets of attention and a little imagination can take us a long way, with simple everyday resources. By way of further illustration, Figure 7.1 illustrates some ways that features of attention might come into play while we are teaching children the concrete processes of counting.

Internal factors affecting attention

People in the same circumstances often have very different responses to the same stimuli; these partly reflect differences in disposition. These effects can be especially important or exaggerated when children have learning difficulties. There are a number of different internal factors that affect children's abilities to focus and maintain attention.

- **Interest** – Events in which we have already gained interest are likely to attract us. So effective cues that prepare and promote positive interest are important. Attitudes and prejudices also affect the extent to which we are drawn to take heed, re-emphasising the need to promote attitudes of interest and curiosity, but also highlighting the need to ensure that students are confident about subject material. Many people, whether or not they have special needs, are predisposed to think that mathematics is a subject that they will fail at, because they think of it as abstract and removed from the reality of their lives. It is

| Intensity | Sometimes use a small torch to point to objects in turn. |
|---|---|
| | Vary the intensity of volume and vocal tones to draw attention to the last word in a number sequence. |
| | Or if you are using modelling technique and guiding a child's finger pointing to counting objects, increase the emphasis of motion, rhythm or pressure when reaching the last object. Together these techniques will provide non-verbal signals giving incidental support to the importance of the last item or number and help children develop understanding of the cardinal principle (see Chapter 11). |
| **Novelty** | Do not restrict yourself to 'counting apparatus', use novel items that attract children's attention. |
| | Everyday items, toys, and stimulating events, like the ball in the biscuit tin, add novelty to focus attention. Nasty plastic fingers are available in the shops around Hallowe'en; even a pink washing up glove can add some freshness to finger counting occasionally. Older children might like to count football cards, lipsticks, or, if you are really brave, eggs. |
| | A variety of real objects also puts across the idea that anything can be counted, as well as helping to break away from the kind of ritual that Mandy displayed in Chapter 6. |
| **Distribution of stimuli** | Young children developing their knowledge of the sequence of count words use the rhythmn and intonation in rhymes to maintain attention and provide memory prompts. When children have learning difficulties and associated coordination problems the process of pointing and coordinated production of count words can become slow and lose the kind of attention spark and memory power that the rhymes give. Even though with older children it is not appropriate to use childish rhymes, we can make sure that the sequence of count words do not sink into a forgettable dirge, by linking intonation and rhythm. Where children have particular difficulties pointing or tracking we need to be aware of the physical distribution of objects being counted, arranging them to alleviate the physical or perceptual hitches and so enable a more stimulating vocal sequence. |
| **Colour** | Use attractively coloured objects that contrast well with backgrounds. Where appropriate use different colours to emphasise different groups, but also remember that sometimes children may not understand why you are asking them to count. Bear in mind that they may be attending to sorting by colour, not thinking of quantity. |
| **High sounds** | Vary the intonation you use when modelling counting. |
| | Use rising intonation to attract attention to important numbers, e.g. the last number of the first group when counting on to a second group then the answer. This emphasises the temporary and the final cardinal number. |
| **Conditioning** | Sometimes use familiar objects or pictures to raise interest in counting. |
| | Items like individual pictures of their family members, real items of food, desired models of footballers, etc., can always raise the level of attention that children are willing to pay. |
| **Cues** | Children have to coordinate noticing each item in turn with assigning it a number name. They use their own physical cues in the form of pointing, but there is wide potential for mistakes and teachers' physical and verbal clues can play a very large part in maintaining pace and providing detail for the learner to absorb within the counting process. |
| | • Coordinated verbal and pointing can help synchronise the start of a child's counting sequence. |
| | • While the motion of pointing cues can carry a child's attention along, the array of objects and emphatic motions can help with the establishment of sequential sound making. Cues like this do not have to be with fingers – various things can be used to add interest and promote attention to pointing (puppets, torches etc.). |

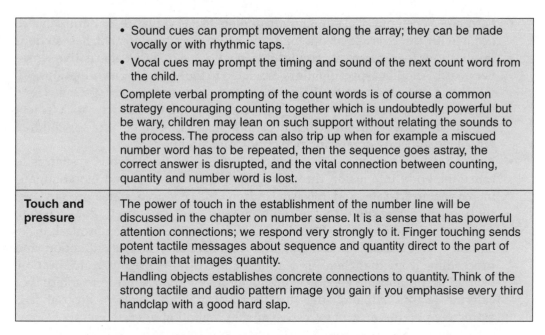

| | |
|---|---|
| | • Sound cues can prompt movement along the array; they can be made vocally or with rhythmic taps. |
| | • Vocal cues may prompt the timing and sound of the next count word from the child. |
| | Complete verbal prompting of the count words is of course a common strategy encouraging counting together which is undoubtedly powerful but be wary, children may lean on such support without relating the sounds to the process. The process can also trip up when for example a miscued number word has to be repeated, then the sequence goes astray, the correct answer is disrupted, and the vital connection between counting, quantity and number word is lost. |
| **Touch and pressure** | The power of touch in the establishment of the number line will be discussed in the chapter on number sense. It is a sense that has powerful attention connections; we respond very strongly to it. Finger touching sends potent tactile messages about sequence and quantity direct to the part of the brain that images quantity. |
| | Handling objects establishes concrete connections to quantity. Think of the strong tactile and audio pattern image you gain if you emphasise every third handclap with a good hard slap. |

**Figure 7.1** Some effects and applications of different facets of attention when teaching children to count

important that we organise teaching and learning experiences that build upon the reality of our pupils' lives, needs and existing skills. The mathematical experiences that we offer need to be relevant to both their learning level and their age. This is a challenge, particularly where teenage pupils are still working towards early levels of skill. Though they may be at early stages of cognitive development they are nevertheless teenagers, and have teenage emotions, sentiments and attitudes, and if we wish to gain their attention and motivate them we need to find teaching materials and strategies that are appropriate to their ages and attitudes. We should use images from magazines, use teenage items for counting, and incorporate our numeracy lesson into practical activities and life events.

- **Physical or social deprivation** – Extreme deprivation can lead to excessive orientation towards the satisfaction of the deprived need. While this factor may generally be considered to relate to basic drives such as hunger, a reflection of it may be observed when sensory difficulties or autistic tendencies lead children to focus on some needs obsessively which make it very difficult for them to attend to appropriate learning experiences.

Both autistic children and epileptic children are frequently prescribed drugs that may ameliorate their conditions, but sometimes side-effects can be disruptive to attention. Children with profound physical disabilities may experience extreme frustration when their attention processes are disrupted by sensory deprivation or continual pain. They may also suffer from deprivation in the sense that they are denied many sensory signals that many of us take for granted; for example, the feelings from the soles of our feet as we stand and walk that tell us so much about our balance and motion, and contribute to our tactile and vestibulary understanding of rhythm and pattern, frequency. Experiences of foot massage may offer them some compensatory experience, but if done insensitively it may equally be very overwhelming, and generate tactile defensive responses.

- **Fatigue** – When physical energies are depleted so is vigilance. Fatigue can also occur with the overuse of one or some senses, a situation that has obvious implications for sensory impaired children who need to work alternative senses very hard. Another aspect of fatigue is related to the amount of information with which we can cope without being swamped; over-stimulation, giving rise to high levels of arousal (see below), can lead to losing the capacity for efficient allocation of attention – a vicious cycle that needs careful balance for children who have difficulty organising perception and attention.

- **Arousal** – In response to stimulation a function of the nervous system is to rouse the body into action through releasing energy in stored blood sugars, increasing heart rate, and releasing adrenaline. Aroused states are survival routines, hypersensitive to the environment, and are closely connected to anxiety, fear and anger. Performance improves with increasing arousal, up to a point. While a basic threshold of arousal is needed to activate attention, and proceeding from that there is a scale of usefully increasing concentration, beyond an optimum level however, which may vary according to internal or external factors, attention deteriorates until at high levels of arousal it is extremely poor because of excessive anxiety, agitation or excitement.

  There is a wide spectrum of difficulties that relate to arousal, that result in children having problems integrating and processing sensory input. At one end of the scale we may have children who are under-sensitive to sensory stimulus, who need large amounts of stimulation to generate attention. While at the other end of the scale there are children who are hyper-reactive to stimulus, who will suffer from anxiety and agitation generated by high levels of arousal. Some implications of these effects are discussed below.

- **Attention needs** – The extent to which a child is driven by curiosity, the desire to explore and manipulate, are all states that are clearly influential in the generation of attention. Curiosity is a constructive response to stimulation and is a driving force in child development. However, the constructive aspects of curiosity, which lead to exploratory acts, are disturbed when children are under- or over-reactive to stimuli as discussed above.

  Under-reactive children will not be triggered to follow the threads of changing stimulus that maintain exploratory curiosity, while high levels of arousal experienced by children hypersensitive to sensory stimulation create anxiety that results in fragmented concentration. The range of what curiosity is applied to is also suppressed by some of these children as a result of the sensory defensive behaviours mentioned in Chapter 5 on Sensation, and expanded on below. Some but not all children who suffer from visual impairment are tactile defensive as a result of anxiety about mobility within their environment. Both the neurally impaired children and the visually impaired who suffer tactile defensive feelings tend to seek secure areas and close themselves into secure worlds rather than reach out curiously. They need security before we can nurture curiosity.

- **Expectation** – This has a two-handed influence upon attention. On the one hand attention is readily drawn towards familiar events, while on the other hand attention is heightened when events are unexpected. There is a balancing act in the provision of learning activities and materials, between using the familiar to set a comfortable learning zone that relates the learner to established perceptual sets, and drawing in new materials and events that heighten arousal and demand accommodation that reinforces or may change existing knowledge.

- **Personality** – Many behavioural distinctions can be drawn between introverted and extroverted learners, and these may be exaggerated when pupils have additional learning difficulties. The sensory threshold required to stimulate introverts is generally lower than for extroverts, though this may be at odds when the introversion is a result of under-reaction to sensory stimulus. Extroverted children need stronger stimulus to draw their attention, and more involuntary rest pauses to maintain concentration. They also accumulate reticence to continuing repetitive tasks; where sustained attention is required they are more likely to wither and become distracted, they need breaks and changes that refresh the novelty value of stimulus.

## When there are difficulties with attention

We need to understand and apply the principles of attention for all our pupils. Their physical and learning disabilities will affect their effective use of attention, and some aspects have been hinted at above. However, one particular group of pupils has cropped up recurrently in this chapter. They are children who have difficulty integrating sensory processing, some of whom would be described as being on the Autistic Continuum. They may be either under- or over-reactive to stimuli to some degree. This will affect their ability to select and organise what their senses receive. Under-reactive children will need large stimuli to attract their attention, they will miss clues and need lots of time to respond. Their kinaesthetic/vestibular and motor development may be delayed, resulting in poor mobility, navigation, and manipulation skills. These children will not be confident in movement and may be defensive about physical exploration in ways that will hold up the mature understanding of space, form and shape. While for much of the time such children may seem slow to respond, at times they may have sudden outbursts because they lack ability to regulate the flow of stimulus and suddenly stimulation might become too much.

At the other end of the spectrum over-reactive children will find that the environment bombards them with more stimuli than they can cope with and they may adopt strategies which are characteristic of children on the autistic spectrum to reduce or divert stimulus. Such children may for example be unable to ignore some of the stimulus of wearing clothes and may continually fidget or pick at and destroy garments, or divest themselves of clothing. On the other hand, there are those who are hypersensitive to touch who may layer clothing on, to protect their skin from random tactile contacts; they may pull their hoods or jumpers up over their heads, or wrap themselves in blankets, to reduce their world to a cocoon, to minimise undesired visual stimulation and to feel the calming inhibitory effects of deep touch receptors, rather than the alerting effects of light touch.

Paradoxically they may also sometimes indulge in obsessive looking at items of seemingly irrelevant fascination, or become compulsively involved in rhythmic sound or motion activities. Children who are hypersensitive to auditory stimuli often express high anxiety about things like vacuum cleaners or balloons, and likewise at other times may display obsessive interests. Sometimes children engage in alternative behaviours such as tapping their teeth, twirling and flapping to self stimulate obsessively, so that they can block out the myriad of other signals, which overload them and create anxiety. Other strategies are to find spaces where they can exclude or limit other people and feel secure, like corners where they can monitor other people's approaches, or toilets where space is limited and the decorative stimulation is bland.

These and similar strategies disrupt the well-balanced and integrated access to stimuli relating to quantities, space and time that is necessary to develop well rounded mathematical concepts. I put it this way because there are many examples of such children developing very high levels of isolated skills, for example, a child who may name written numerals even to 35,776 and yet be unable to know that three children need three cups to drink from.

Recent years have seen a significant growth in understanding of appropriate ways to communicate and teach autistic children, and it would appear there is consensus that different approaches work for different children. Though there is insufficient space here to explore approaches thoroughly, there are references that may be useful, including Aarons and Gittens (1999), and an American perspective giving an overview of programmes such as Picture Exchange Communication System (PECS), Applied Behavioural Analysis (ABA) and TEACCH methods as described by Quinn and Malone (2000).

We cannot remove the disabilities that deeply affect these children but we can mitigate the effects of the environment in which we teach them. We noted earlier that both visually and neurally impaired children needed areas where they could shelter from extraneous stimulation and keep their arousal anxieties at more tolerable levels. This may be difficult in classrooms that provide for a wide range of learners who may be noisy communicators, or frequently involved in sensory motor learning activities, which are noisy. However, for some parts of the autistic child's numeracy lesson we need to strive to create some areas of the classroom that are quiet, whatever you want to call them, workstations or mini environments, where stimuli can be controlled. We also need to ensure that areas of display are well defined, surrounded by neutral areas to avoid becoming mingled with other stimuli. We need to enter these environments and present stimuli in ways that fall within the children's comfort zone of processing so that they are not roused to high anxiety levels and can usefully observe, and connect stimuli. Bearing in mind the anxieties caused by direct communication, it may be useful to sit next to rather than opposite, and to model activities in ways that draw their interest, rather than present them with things you seem to expect them to do. An interesting approach might be to use the kind of personal dialogue that you might use internally when trying to complete a difficult task; such egocentric or self-directive speech is natural to young children, and don't deny you use it – thinking aloud when there is no one around. It is non-demanding but informative. Donna Williams* (1992), an autistic girl, describes the effectiveness of 'speaking through objects' in the epilogue of her remarkable autobiography, *Nobody Nowhere*. Specific stimuli and language can be related by the teacher or support worker in these ways, as individual teaching during the middle part of the daily mathematics lesson. One to one may not need to last the whole period; the child may pick up on the modelling and continue the exploration or practice.

However there is also a place within the daily numeracy lesson for whole-class and group teaching, where children exercise and share their knowledge about quantities, space, shape and changing events, and so develop their understanding of social maths. To learn to participate in this sharing knowledge about things and quantities is an important dimension of all our lives, and it is just as valuable as it is difficult for children with autistic predispositions. Though I am advocating the involvement of such children in the starter and plenary sessions of the daily numeracy lesson I am not underestimating the difficulty, or the adaptations that have to be made to attract them. One secret of success is seduction, indirect temptation and fascination. It is not always necessary to be sitting with the group to be attending, maybe that is something we need to work towards, and maybe the fascination of numbers expressed in patterns of sounds and activities could be a powerful aid to promoting involvement in that vital social skill. Children who are tempted to pay remote attention from across the room can be obliquely tempted to come a little way towards us, if the commentary and activities have some dimension that interests them. Remember, events that include changing quantities and shapes have an intrinsic fascination for many. So starter and plenary sessions for special pupils need attractive active dimensions, the language used needs to be modulated in rhythm and tone to attract, and highlight the magic of reality. On the other hand, pupils with attention difficulties need to be drawn to the stimuli so that they feel they are in control, and not overloaded. Donna Williams' thoughts on this situation were that she always felt interactions should be initiated by herself, or at least she should have a choice, but she acknowledged that young children needed to be challenged to learn that they can choose. Though it went against the grain of her natural inclinations she recommended that to draw autistic children into interactions strong, persistent, sensitive, though impersonal approaches were necessary. These thoughts could be the start of a lengthy discussion and this chapter needs to draw to an end so I will leave you with some more of Donna's thoughts. She maintains that symbolic gestures and actions were important ways of indirectly expressing her feelings. They were ways of representing things she felt so strongly about that ' in the riddle-like nature of my ironic trap' she dared not directly say. In her book she describes what some of the actions and gestures meant to her. I do not know if it is significant, but the first three of the twenty things she describes relate to activities that connect to mathematics, perhaps justifying my contention that we may be able to find things that fascinate such students and draw them into our lessons. I quote her words because for me they have resonance and I want to provoke your thoughts.

*1. The matching or pairing of objects*
Making connections between things, showing relations between two or more things can exist. Seeing this objectified through objects in the most concrete and undeniable way; seeing this and creating it again and again gave me hope that if the concept was possible, then it would one day be possible to feel and accept these relationships in 'the world'. I was always within this world of objects.

*2. The ordering of objects and symbols*
Proving that belonging exists and giving myself hope that one day I, too, could one day feel this same special and undeniable place where I, too, fitted and belonged in 'the world'. Also creating order and thereby making this symbolic representation of 'the world' more comprehensible.

*3. Patterns*
Continuity. The reassurance that things will stay the same long enough to grasp an undeniable guaranteed place where I, too fitted in and belonged in the complex situation around me. Surrounding circles or border lines, these are set up as a means of protection from invasion from that which exists outside, in 'the world'.

It strikes me that though Donna was not talking about maths, within her feelings about matching, ordering and pattern, there were things that show us how deeply elemental mathematics contributes our understanding of the world: although in a different way for Donna, like Einstein feeling mathematics was a part of thinking.

# 8 Number sense

## Returning to number sense

In Chapter 2 we discussed how neurologists and psychologists have proposed that we have a sense of numerosity. Although not a sense in the same way as sight or hearing, it provides us with a foundation and processes through which we develop the whole of our mathematical knowledge. The proposals that they describe are of great interest to those of us who are working with children who are at the early stages of learning. To understand their learning needs we need to take ourselves back to learning experiences that we take for granted, for example the powerful sense of 'one' that comes from holding a single item in one palm, and how different it is when both hands are occupied – three is too many to hold, and is therefore a beginning of the concept of 'many'.

While we must accept that some children's learning difficulties may actually stem from some shortcomings of their number sense, it is also likely that knowledge about how it works and familiarity with the ideas that relate to it might offer us teaching strategies through which we can help evolve their sense of numerosity and link it to the experiences they encounter, enabling them to access learning about fundamental mathematics.

### Specialised circuits

So we need to know what number sense is and how it contributes to our learning. Briefly, Brian Butterworth (1999) proposes that there are sets of circuits in areas in the rear part of the brain, known as the parietal lobe, which have functions that are at the core of our numerical abilities. The circuits are usually functioning from the first days of our lives and give very young infants the capacity to use visual or other sensory information to recognise the 'numerosity' of a group of up to three or four items. Dehaene suggests that we have an inclination to particularly notice and anticipate accumulation, so we are very interested when things are added to groups.

In another part of the left parietal lobe there are other circuits that deal with spatial orientation, and we use these circuits to develop and hold mental representations of the order of quantities. Picture in your mind's eye the sequence of numbers from one onwards: does it form a line, which way does it go? These areas also relate to finger control, and Butterworth proposes that there are interrelations between the circuits, so that the representations of quantities we form in our brain are connected to spatial and tactile representations, and patterns that we make with our fingers. Interplay between all these sets of circuits helps children to develop ideas about quantities, and their representation.

We know that infants can identify small groups because Karen Wynn (1992) observed that they respond to changes in the numerosity of groups by showing increased vigilance. This ability to immediately recognise the size of a group without counting is known as 'subitising', a process of perceiving, remembering and comparing, that is strongly related to the perceptual processes of connecting and grouping stimuli that we discussed in Chapter 6. It stays with us and is commonly illustrated in our ability to identify the group that comes up when a dice is rolled. It may be of interest to note that in Wynn's experiments children's ability to notice and compare the size of groups was not limited to visual items; they showed the same renewal of attention when groups of sounds or actions were changed. Butterworth concludes from this that infants had an interest in enumerating anything they could think of as a separate entity. For those of us who work with children with sensory difficulties this confirms that we can help build their concepts of number through alternative sensory channels, counting sounds or touches.

Other observations by Wynn tie in with Dehaene's idea of the brain being particularly tuned to notice accumulations. They suggest that very young children possess 'arithmetical expectations' in that they are able to anticipate the increase or decrease effects of adding or taking items away from a small group. Again they show increased vigilance if their expectations are not met. Together these abilities indicate to us that infants can:

- compare numerosities;
- select the larger of two;
- have a sense of their order by size.

These abilities would suggest that even at a very early age children have an emergent mental representation of a number line. It seems probable that its range may be limited, only up to three, but with an awareness of 'more than three'. We should bear in mind that at this stage recognising numerosity is recognising quantities, not yet counting. In Chapter 11 we will discuss the importance of fingers as first symbols in the processes of learning counting. Butterworth calls the brain circuitry that provides these processes 'The Number Module'. He suggests that children develop their mathematical ideas when the experience they gather using their number module interacts with cultural stimulus around them, provided by their observation of events, what others do and say, and teaching, as represented in Figure 8.1. This is the fundamental beginning of understanding numbers and without it we would not be able to lead our practical daily lives, nor would mathematics ever fly to its more abstract heights.

### Developing a universal characteristic

Other mammals and birds have been shown to share with us the instinctual perception and ability to compare and memorise small quantities, skills that are useful in the course of survival. Connecting these skills to the power of language, by attaching symbolic names to quantities, is the strategy that has enabled humans to extend their abilities beyond the elementary powers of the number module.

Different cultures have developed very different languages. However, the writings of Brian Butterworth and Stanislas Dehaene illustrate many ways in which the number module has been globally important. All cultures have developed systems of counting that are remarkably similar, and they date back to pre history. Using words rather than relying upon objects to represent quantities was a big step forward, and even in this process there is common ground in that number names have commonly been drawn from body parts, particularly fingers. We might conclude that the development of children's mathematical abilities reflects the development of mathematics itself, both evolving from a universal interest in quantities and how they change. From the mists of time humans have used their fingers as markers to memorise and order numerosities and they have been instrumental tools that have enabled us to extend our inborn perceptions of quantity into number systems.

*Pointing*

We noted earlier how children have a propensity to group and enumerate anything they can think of as a separate entity, and herein is perhaps the first link between language and mathematics, pointing. The role of index finger pointing and coordinated sound making is well documented as a vital element in language development (Butterworth, G. 1998). It is the means by which we indicate communicative intention and focus the attention that we share with other people; it is also the means by which we learn to link objects to words. As well as these things, pointing is a unique and powerful way to highlight and sense individualisation, or one-ness. According to John Locke writing in 1690 about the arithmetic achieved by Amazonian natives, we construct the idea of each number from the idea of 'one', which he refers to as 'the most universal idea that we have' (Butterworth, B. 1999). In the light of our earlier discussion concerning the neurological connections between fingers and the area of our brain where we make and use internal representations of number, we may realise how important pointing is to the development of internal representations that contribute to helping us develop and use our concept of 'one'.

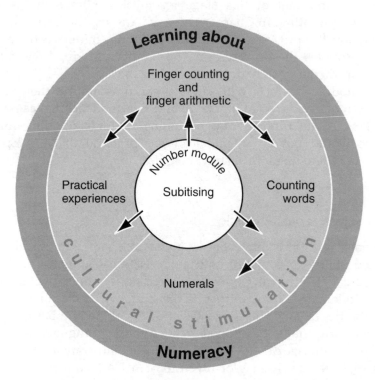

How the components of cultural stimulus interact and work with the number module

**Figure 8.1**  The Number Module and cultural influences on learning about number (adapted from Butterworth, B. (1999))

*Beyond one*

Pointing at one item denotes its individuality, pointing at items in turn expresses accumulation. The connection of that accumulation to the language of number is an important step that links subitising and counting in the child's mind. Typical infants are able to recognise and compare numerosities up to three via their natural number sense, while encountering and experiencing the counting behaviour of other people introduces them to number words for one, two and three. The child gradually confirms by recognising equivalences that specific words are used to describe each of the particular quantities that they subitise. This knowledge is also consolidated by the use of fingers, which we have noted are connected to the areas of the brain that make spatial representation. So one, two and three are not only put in order on the fingers but also form a mental representation, which will extend to become their internal representation number line. We will see more detail about how the child develops further concepts of numbers and the importance of finger manipulation and counting in Chapters 11 and 12 when we contemplate processes of cognitive learning, and learning to count.

## Number sense and the special needs curriculum

The conventional maths curriculum assumes that children have absorbed a great deal of fundamental mathematical knowledge before they start school; teaching programmes for Reception children anticipate that they will say and use number names in order and count reliably within the Reception year. These skills are beyond the reach of many pupils with severe or profound learning difficulties, and in the past we have failed to describe mathematical learning that is appropriate for them. Even the recent P levels, produced by the QCA in 1998 to describe early learning targets, assumed that for early development (levels P1 to P3) it was not necessary to describe mathematical content. The notions of 'number sense', expressed for us by neuro-scientists interested in the most fundamental and yet the most complex aspects of how humans work, show us that from the first days of children's lives they are interested in quantities, and how they change. From these simple beginnings there is a course of experience and learning through which children develop their mathematical skills. Mathematics does not, as Piaget or Bertrand Russell proposed, wait for logic. Before it develops, mathematics is in the rhythm of our lives and it starts at the beginning. Why should the curriculum start anywhere else? Typical children progress so fluently through the essential experiences upon which fundamental mathematics is built that we may take their learning for granted. But such experiences are the content of mathematical learning that special pupils need to focus on and which previous curricula have failed to reach. With an awareness of the learning involved in number sense, and the knowledge gained from other recent research into how children learn to count, special teachers will be able to enhance approaches to the National Curriculum and Numeracy Strategy, to provide a mathematics curriculum appropriate for very special pupils.

In the past special curriculum approaches have divided much early learning into categories such as cognitive development, or gross or fine motor skills, or communication skills, and such categories were separated from mathematics until children could grasp and use numbers. Now we see that typically children are learning about quantities and numbers from very early days. Mathematics is a subject that they learn from even at the earliest stages of their lives. Some of the experiences that help them develop the use of their senses and their powers of perception and attention have distinctly mathematical flavours and purposes, involving quantity, space and time. For example, when a child uses fine coordination to point and touch objects it is sometimes for the purpose of knowing or showing, or feeling 'how many'.

It is difficult for us to comprehend that children may not understand what seem to us to be innate concepts. Many children who have special needs do not communicate with us clearly about quantities, and yet because it is so fundamental to us we may still assume that they understand the linear progression of accumulating quantity, and are able to understand us when we ask which is 'more'. We cannot, however, make these assumptions and we need to focus our appraisal of their needs more closely to detect at what level their number sense may need support. We may find they need opportunities to experience accumulation or have their attention brought to equivalences; they may need to learn to touch and point, or to make tactile or mental images. There are a host of such experiences that typical infants revel in, and learn from, but which special children may not cope with or be able to organise into learning. There is a wealth of sensory learning to be organised in order to understand the elements of quantity, space, shape and time, and this learning is the bedrock that is usually laid even before children have language. To develop their number sense children need to encounter and respond to fundamental experiences.

When children have emergent language and start to develop counting beyond the limitation of their number sense it is important for them to encounter and experience the counting of small collections to consolidate the connection between subitising and naming, and also to confirm in their minds that counting is a way of establishing numerosity. The connection between subitising and naming illustrates to children that there is

- a sequence of accumulation;
- particular relations of quantity between number name words;
- a stable order of their occurrence.

These ideas help children to develop the idea of a number line, as a linear progression of accumulation, and given this concept children are gradually able to add new numbers infinitely. We will return again to these themes when we review research into how children learn to count and when we consider appropriate curriculum content for children at different levels of ability.

# Part Three

# The processes of learning – phases of cognition

## 9 Cognition – unfolding phases and processes of learning

### The mind of the child

The newborn child is confronted with a sea of sensation and in the course of life's learning begins making sense of it all. Children usually do this with much greater speed than psychologists once believed. We now know that in the very first days children can discern between smaller and greater quantities, and by six months show a beginning awareness of the permanence of number and simple laws (Wynn 1992). From such beginnings we develop all that characterises the adult mathematical mind.

The areas of the brain that build up associations are the last to develop, and as they do so the child's mental abilities gush forward (Chugani and Phelps 1986). The brain – our neural hardware – and the mind – our cognitive software – develop together. If we are to understand learning we need to understand how the mind of the child works.

### Ideas about the pattern of child development

*Two important ideas – schemas and stages*
The Swiss psychologist, Jean Piaget, was the first person to establish that the child's mind is not a miniature of the adult. Nowadays we culturally accept this idea but we still sometimes overlook it when we teach; or when our children fail to respond to our commands, by misunderstanding in particularly exasperating ways. Two ideas that Piaget proposed about the nature of children's development are particularly important for us to understand.

### Schema

The driving force behind intellectual development is our incessant desire to make sense of our experience. In this pursuit the maturing brain collects and groups ideas from experience to form concepts, which Piaget called schemas. The schemes work at physical and mental levels, and by the time we are adults we have developed and redeveloped thousands of them, from practical actions like waving goodbye or buttering toast, practical ideas like trajectory, to intellectual, social or emotional concepts like being in love. Our schemes do not stay the same; hopefully we improve our ideas and ways of doing things. Piaget proposed two ideas about how we adjust our schemes; he called these the processes of Assimilation and Accommodation. First, we interpret new experiences in the light of our current understanding – that is, we match it to our scheme of things. Piaget described this as 'assimilating experience'. So having a simple scheme for a cat a toddler might call all four-legged creatures Pussy. However we adjust – or 'accommodate' – our schemes to fit particulars of new experiences, just as the child soon learns that the original cat schema was too broad and refines their understanding of the category. As children interact with the world they build and adapt their understanding of it. Hopefully we

## Piaget's framework
## Stages of cognitive development

| **Sensory motor stage** (See Part Two and Chapter 10) | | |
|---|---|---|
| Typical age range | Description of stage | Developmental milestones |
| Birth to nearly two years | Experience of the world through senses and actions. Looking, touching, mouthing, moving. | • Grasping, handling<br>• Tracking<br>• Object permanence<br>• Stranger anxiety<br>• Mobility |
| **Pre-operational phase** (See Chapter 11) | | |
| About two to six years | Preparation for concrete operations<br>From pre-conceptual to intuitive thinking | Developmental milestones |
| | Initially pre-conceptual thinking.<br>Starting to represent things with words and images.<br>Develop intuitive thinking but still lacking logical reasoning.<br>*(A time for envisioning quantities and beginning to learn to count)* | • Egocentrism<br>*(The world revolves around 'me')*<br>• Beginning Theory of Mind<br>• Intuitive concepts<br>• Ability to pretend |
| **Concrete operational stage** (See Chapter 12) | | |
| About seven to eleven years | Description of stage | Developmental milestones |
| | Thinking logically but only about concrete events, grasping concrete analogies, and performing arithmetical operations. | Conservation<br>Mathematical transformations |
| **Formal operational stage** | | |
| About twelve through to adulthood | Description of stage | Developmental milestones |
| | Abstract reasoning. | Potential for mature moral reasoning |
| Piaget envisaged development as following stages. Later researchers have found that children have some abilities much earlier than Piaget thought, and suggest that progress is much smoother with a great deal of overlap and interplay between stages. Spiral links in this diagram suggest anticipation and revisitation between stages. | | |

**Figure 9.1** Piaget's framework for stages of cognitive development (adapted)

all carry on assimilating and accommodating for the rest of our days. Later we will take a closer look at some of the schema that young children develop and practise that pertain to their developing understandings of quantity, space and time.

**Stages**

Though many have criticised detail, or refined his ideas, the Piaget framework has been the scaffolding from which modern understanding of children's learning has been built. He believed that the child's mind developed in a series of stages in an upward progression from newborn reflexes to adult abstract reasoning (Piaget and Inhelder 1969). The stages that he proposed are outlined, though slightly adapted, in Figure 9.1. Later studies have revealed that human cognition does unfold in the sequence that Piaget proposed (Segall *et al.* 1990) but have also revealed the beginnings of each type of thinking in children at earlier ages (Donaldson, M. 1978). Present day interpretations emphasise a very flexible view of stages, recognising a good deal of overlap, which in effect means that progress through stages is evolutionary and not a matter of sudden leaps. Modern psychologists have assimilated Piaget's theories and accommodated new information into them. The sequences of development that he proposed offer a framework which we will use as a reference and as a framework for discussing more recent understandings about child development and how they apply to our special children.

We start with the sensory and motor learning that characterises the very early development of exploring, manipulating and moving. Children pass from exploration and thought dominated by immediate perceptions, through a period of understanding things in real terms (concrete operations), and gradually develop the ability to make mental representations that enable them to think of things that are not present and can be combined as abstract ideas. Eventually children reach the level Piaget called formal operations, which is the realm of reasoning and abstract thinking. (The mathematics curriculum for children who are capable of formal operations is described in the National Curriculum and the Numeracy Strategy.)

During their school lives the special children with whom this book is concerned are mostly spread across the earlier levels of these stages. Many aspects of the learning of some of our more profoundly disadvantaged pupils may remain predominantly in the realm of sensory motor learning for many years, or even their whole life. Many students will show signs of functioning in different stages at the same time; in different situations they may seem to grasp things and function at different levels. So, though we are going to use Piaget's structure to give us a framework to think about appropriate learning activities and teaching strategies, we should never forget that we need to be flexible in our attitude to it.

# 10  Sensory motor learning

## Learning to explore

By five months a child can intercept a moving object, by nine months adjust the width and orientation of their grasp to match the size and shape of objects they intend to pick up. Some complex, practical mathematical calculations have been taking place.

As children become able to coordinate the interaction of their sensory and physical abilities, there is more than physical development at stake. They reach out to the world for stimulation and lay down important foundations of information gathering. From these beginnings wider skills develop, stimulating communication and awareness that things still exist even when out of sight. This simple notion is an embarkation on the journey towards reasoning and abstract thought. Some phases of this journey that are driven by curiosity are described in Figure 10.1. Although it does not stick rigidly to Piaget's described stages, this figure does describe behaviours that occur as children progress through them. It also draws on observations of developmental behaviours of infants made by Uzgiris and Hunt (1975). Many publications that relate to curriculum development and recording for pupils with severe or profound learning difficulties also reflect this structure, e.g. the 'P' scales within the Target Setting for Special Schools document issued by QCA (1998), and the EQUALS' Baseline (1998) assessment and PMLD curriculum documents (1999).

## Stages within stages

From the day of birth to nearly two, infants understand their world through sensory interaction with objects; this is a period when children learn to coordinate and use their senses and learn to move and manipulate things (*motor development*). This is a fantastic period of development, during which we develop many skills that are so simple that we take them for granted, but so important that without them we would have no civilisation. We can look into it deeper and deeper, there are stages within the stages, and the following paragraphs outline the broad sequence of events. Though they are represented as a hierarchy, in reality there are elements of overlap and flexibility in the actual sequences in which children approach, practise and master activities and skills. At first Piaget seems to focus his descriptions on children's movements, and the names he uses, 'primary, secondary and tertiary circular responses', sound complicated. Though I risk simplifying his important insights, I think it is worth setting aside the jargon for a moment to describe what children do in more everyday language. Starting from their first reflex responses, children develop increasingly controlled movements of their limbs, and these tend to be circular movements. Piaget noticed three phases through which the first reflex actions, such as the instinctive curling grasp, develop through extending and combining circular movements, to become more sophisticated, reaching, holding and manipulating skills, all progressing to enable our mobility and walking. Figure 10.1, 'Some early phases of exploration', illustrates stages in the development and how children's movements help them develop towards skills that have wider implications than manipulation and movement alone.

### Reflex motions

During the first months this interaction takes place through very simple schema: looking, listening, grasping, touching, mouthing and moving. Their actions are reflex and seem to move to any thing that attracts. At this early stage children seem unaware that anything can exist outside the realm of their gaze. Out of sight is out of mind; they are unaware that objects have permanence.

### Primary circular reactions

Gradually the child's limb movements gain some pattern and take up cyclic movements; they may combine movements, for example, place a thumb in the mouth. These are *primary circular movements*, and they give us a clue of the existence of primitive memories. They are extensions of the reflex activities, that focus within the child's self, not yet purposeful actions. Primary circular reactions are mainly occupied with the practice and assimilation of actions, such as controlling, grasping and reaching, or placing palms together.

### Secondary circular reactions

Usually at about four to eight months new actions begin to appear that have less noticeable connection to reflexes, and the baby seems to visually direct its activities towards objects outside the body; the range of actions rapidly increases, developing new schema, and then improving them, practising and improving visual and motor coordination. These are called *secondary circular reactions* and they are the beginnings of the processes of reaching out to explore objects. At first they are relatively simple schemes that can be indiscriminately applied to any object such as grasping, hitting, shaking; they work towards the use of a two-handed scoop, hand transference and looking at the held objects. Later in this phase, at around seven months, in addition to handling schemes, children may begin to include more complex exploratory manipulations that are differentiated according to the nature of the objects which they are investigating. They include scratching, rubbing, tearing, and crumpling. There are indications that the child is aware that objects have permanence; they look for them because they realise that they may be somewhere to be found.

### Beginning to cause effects and find social dimensions

Between eight and twelve months the child may adopt intentional actions such as dropping and throwing, observing the result. There is every sign in the child's behaviour that these are purposeful movements, directed towards goals. For example, the infant may move things out of the way to obtain a particular toy which implies that schema are being assimilated and accommodated by combining secondary circular reactions, whereas hitherto there had been little sign of accommodation. Some actions reflect social influences, as children make connections like attempting to put the shoe on a doll or putting building bricks together. Socially instigated behaviours may facilitate subsequent attachment of verbal labels to objects.

**Tertiary circular reactions**

From twelve to eighteen months exploration escalates as children become capable of inventing new ways of attaining their ends. Circular motions can be repeated with several variations and *tertiary circular movements* can become complex purposeful sequences. The child may examine objects intently and identify the functional side. They may also begin to extend their powers of cause and effect by deliberately dropping and discarding objects in order to find them again.

**The importance of play**

All of the physical activities that we have described so far have grown from beginnings in reflex activity; there is a growing complexity and the child practises and adapts endlessly. Though many of the activities seem to have practical ends in obtaining things, things are also soon discarded as attention moves on; these processes are commonly regarded as play. Play is a spontaneous activity, common among the young of most higher animals; it satisfies what seems to be an active will to learn which some psychologists have described as cognitive drive. It is exhibited in the ceaseless curiosity, exploration, manipulation and practice that I have described in the processes of sensory motor learning, where it contributes its part in the physical development of the child's body skills, and in developing their understanding of shape, texture, weight, quantity, etc.

At first, as we have observed it in the early stages of the sensory motor period, children's play is solitary. As time progresses children develop towards more social dimensions, as will be evident in the following sections when we consider how children discover cause and effect, and develop the beginnings of reasoning. Initially social play entails playing alongside others, without mixing; later it involves becoming engaged in associative and cooperative play, through which the rules of coexistence are experienced, which gives children the chance to develop social competence and moral sense. We will certainly return to the themes of social play when we discuss the development of children's communication and thinking skills, since these processes also underpin the child's abilities to gather information from other people about things and what is happening in the immediate world around them, including quantities, space and time, and as such are intrinsic in their development of social mathematics.

There have been many debates about how play should be absorbed into the educational structures of teaching, mostly recognising the power of play as a motivational driver of learning, while also acknowledging the need to guide unstructured practice by suitably shaping and ordering materials and experiences to provide focus to learning. The Early Learning Goals, published by the QCA in 1999 to guide practice in the Foundation stage in our schools, restates the importance of the role of the practitioner in supporting and extending play through well-planned environments and activities.

**Discovering and communicating about effect**

Towards the end of the sensory motor period when the onset of language enables children to refer to objects, there are opportunities for even wider applications and development of schema, that have physical, linguistic and mental aspects. The child may refer to objects in their absence. This use of verbal symbolism is paralleled with other forms of symbolisation; toys can represent real things and objects can represent other things, so for example toy bricks can be played with as if they were cars, and the child may be making mental representations of objects. At this point children may begin to appreciate that quantities have names.

Up to this time most activities have involved physical action on concrete objects, but at this point play becomes an important aspect of assimilating meaning. Combining objects and actions with meanings leads children to explore functional uses and solve problems. For example they begin to associate objects with events that might involve a particular object, or seek a particular item to create an event.

Children with communication difficulties often use strategies from this level of understanding for communication, for example when they show you a cup to let you know they want a drink. They may not be able to refer to objects that are not present because they cannot verbally name them: this can be a source of frustrated pointing actions which we need to help them refine into communicative signs.

**Beginnings of reasoning**

When the developing use of language breaks in to become a prominent part of the interactions between sensory and motor activities, some schemas become capable of wider implication. 'Showing' is a complex scheme in which the child uses an object to initiate interaction with another person, the intention being to share attention about it, not necessarily to give it up. 'Imitation' is an example of accommodation, because the child is attempting to modify behaviour to become something or somebody else. 'Deferred imitation', the ability to imitate someone else in his or her absence, shows the ability to form an image of an event, which can be recalled and reproduced in the future.

'Naming' is not only an indication that the object is recognised, but also that it can be symbolised by a name; it is also regarded as a link between activity levels of concrete recognition and symbolic imagery, which is a beginning of abstract thinking.

Mathematics earlier than you think

The descriptions I have given above readily illustrate the steps through which the coordination and skills of physical exploration and manipulation develop. However, although the observable learning that takes place seems to be very much oriented towards physical growth, we would be underestimating the importance of the sensory motor period if we were to think that it was only about the development of motor and manipulative skills. From the very beginning there is another narrative unfolding and we should acknowledge that the developing skills of the sensory motor period move persistently towards a process of exploring, recognising and knowing. The Latin word 'cognito', means to apprehend and it is the origin of the English word to 'recognise'; these roots characterise the meaning of 'cognitive'. Since the sensory motor period is a time during which children learn to explore and recognise, it is therefore a time during which they establish the fundamentals of cognitive learning.

We see early glimpses of cognitive learning, for example as children develop their understanding of Object Permanence, which is a very important concept for understanding numeracy that most observers of child development agree is established at around four and a half months. But there are also the surprising abilities that arise from number sense that we have discussed earlier. We now know from the work of Wynn (1992) that children in the very early days of life recognise when there are differences between quantities. We may debate whether they have been born with this ability, or have learned it, but we can be sure that it is something that they build upon to establish their knowledge of number. Wynn's experiments showed a progressive sophistication in those recognition skills and in the applications of them, as children grew older. She showed that at five months children could anticipate if there should be an increase or decrease when quantities changed.

So we might reasonably assume that during these first six months of life, far from being a time when all learning is about the coordination of senses and movement, there is a lot cognitive learning taking place. The evidence is there, because during that time the children are becoming more sophisticated in their recognition and

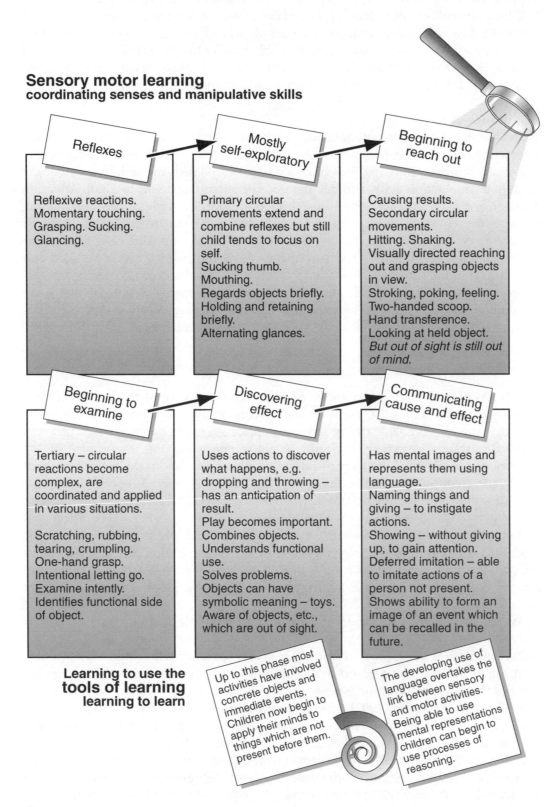

**Figure 10.1**   Some early phases of exploration

anticipation of quantities; there is mathematics earlier than the psychologists and philosophers of the 1960s thought.

There are other features that indicate to us just how wide the range of learning is during this fundamental period. You may have noted, from my text and from Figure 10.1, that as the stages of the sensory motor period progress, the child, who has become an incorrigible examiner of objects, likes to try out actions on objects, discovering effects; but more than this, they discover that people respond to effects, point things out, and tell them things. This begins to lead children towards forms of communication that inform them about the world, and from which they can learn. The child becomes aware of other people's communications in very important ways which we will review in greater detail when we discuss the development of language and thinking in Chapter 11.

So, although this period of learning may be characterised by developing physical activity and manipulation, there is a great deal of other learning associated with the development of exploratory skills. Mental development is evident in cognitive learning that embraces concepts of object permanence and quantity, as well as in children's evident memory for things they have seen before. Awareness of communications that support and inspire exploration is evident in children's reactions and responses. All these aspects of mental and communication development are intertwined with the physical developments that Piaget observed. Physical, cognitive and communication acts are inseparable. They all work together in the development of the child's thinking and activity. So while we easily observe and recognise the growing sophistication of physical movements as children move through the phases of primary, secondary and tertiary circular movements, we should not underestimate the mental developments, including understanding about the changing natures of quantities, shape and space, that are also entwined with those unfolding schema.

## When there are difficulties with sensory motor learning

The learning development, that I have described, which occurs during the sensory motor period involves integrated processes of physical activity, sensory observation and memory. These occur in children's spontaneous play, and are promoted and focused by well-structured environments and activities provided by supportive parents, teachers and other practitioners.

Children with physical, sensory, or cognitive disabilities may be disadvantaged in their natural inclination and ability to play; they may even require encouragement to fire their curiosity, and support in developing exploration and manipulation. In such cases they will require strategies, including compensatory physical experiences and modelling activities, to help them explore. When implementing such strategies we should always remember the spirit of 'play' is spontaneous and exploratory. Our strategies should be stimulating and open to the child's response, in balance with the levels of direction and focus that our teaching objectives suggest, because a primary objective should be to encourage independent curiosity and awareness of the possibilities of exploration. To offer some recompense for limited movement children whose physical difficulties limit compensatory modelling may require supplementary sensory experiences, with elements that emphasise relevant aspects of experiences.

While offering compensatory experiences in our teaching we should remember that it is not just the physical actions of the learners that we are exercising, we are also hoping to strengthen cognitive connections between that physical activity, sensory and perceptual information, memory, thinking and communication skills. So physical experiences should relate to stimuli that attract attention and focus perception. If the focus of the exercise is mathematical we should emphasise communications about the properties and changes in quantity, space and time that are involved.

In the past there has been great deal of focus on physical learning, and patterning processes. Sometimes this emphasis resulted in schools having a 'developmental curriculum' in which motor development was an end in itself. I would not wish to deny the importance of learning to move and handle things, but the curriculum is so much richer, and learning more effective, when reaching and handling encompasses experiencing and commenting on the quality and excitement of our environment. To help our children to develop an understanding of the world they move in it is important that their movements explore and relate to an environment rich in stimulation, and this is a dimension that both the Sensory Curriculum espoused so creatively by Flo Longhorn (1988) and subject teaching advocated by the National Curriculum has enabled us to move towards. Through this movement we have gained a curriculum vision that is much wider, and offers much more opportunity than the behaviourist models we started from in the 1970s.

Many physical activities of the sensory motor period can be seen to relate directly to mathematical concepts; for example, holding a balloon with both hands has obvious connections to experience of space, shape, etc. However, there are also other subtler implications; for example, a driving force of learning is cerebral patterning generated by primary and secondary circular movements – thus the exploration of space itself has a role in cerebral development. When we consider the deep-seated limitations to learning that occur when pupils have sensory and physical difficulties, there is good reason for including sensory motor activities including manipulation, movement, and focusing attention on the exploration of size, shape, weight, etc., as part of the mathematics curriculum for very special children. These activities are the practical expressions of the early learning levels described by the QCA in the P levels that illustrate steps of learning that progress towards Level One of the National Curriculum.

## Returning to schema

Looking in detail at children's movements and manipulations we can see some interesting patterns in the way they move, play with and combine things. An awareness of these can be very useful to us. So we return to the idea of schema, that was remarked upon in Chapter 9. They are patterns of behaviour and thinking that we link together to become useful activities. As we discussed earlier, Piaget's observations showed how the reflex actions that children are born with are soon combined and organised into purposeful patterns he called schema. Once a schema has been developed it can be applied in other situations. Different schemas become integrated, and the child modifies them to meet requirements. This process is evident in the period of tertiary circular actions, when lots of different movements are combined to make useful manipulation skills. But this is not just physical development because sensory and mental memories are generated by the experiences, and perhaps for some children the language associated with them. When the child can remember actions and visualisations internally using memory, imagery or symbolic language they can use *representational schema* – combinations of ideas.

We might observe children's schema as they manipulate objects, or make drawings, we might see them in their movements or gestures, but what is more difficult to envisage is that they are also part of children's internal worlds and concepts. For example, in the transporting schema described below we can see children move things around, and we would easily observe how doing this they may separate or group things together. It is harder to realise that the children may create equivalent internal images of these processes and these are the beginnings of their internal understanding of addition or subtraction.

*Some schema for mathematical learning*
There are some schemas that are clearly related to shape, space and to quantities. Activities that stimulate practice of those schemas may contribute to the child's fund of elementary mathematical experience. In her book *Threads of Thinking* (1999) Cathy Nutbrown identified a rich variety of mathematical ideas being explored by nursery-aged children through schematic activity. These included numbers, sorting, time, matching, quantity, position, estimation, transformation, addition, length, equivalence, distance, symmetry, cause and effect, rotation and trajectory. Schematic activities are built through combinations of a small number of major schemas:

- vertical and horizontal
- circular movements
- enveloping or containing.

As typical children practise each schema they usually seem to have an idea that is the dominant focus of their investigation. Combinations can create or represent many forms of actions and thoughts. Certain schematic patterns recur during different aspects of learning, and when children are in different circumstances. When I first worked on the list below I thought it might be mainly of interest at the earliest levels of learning, but schemas recur in different forms, at different levels in our learning. For example, visual tracking of moving objects is a skill pursued as a practical observation skill by infants, and may be a proficiency that some pupils with profound difficulties need to pursue, while at later levels learning to read requires a tracking of text. It may be useful to consider the application of schema at different levels to provide us with avenues of differentiation.

The following are examples of activities that relate to mathematical learning, which arise from ways in which the three major schemas interact.

### Activities relating to mathematical learning

- **Holding**. To have and to hold, a powerful tactile experience, which grows from that fundamental response of the newborn child that I saw when my daughter wrapped all her tiny fingers around my forefinger. Soon, holding is coordinated with looking, surely one of the experiences from which concept of 'one' springs, along with the awareness of objects that will eventually be a constituent part of object permanence. Then there is one thing in each hand – have you ever seen the bemused delight of a young infant who having something in each hand realises they are fully occupied, and they have great difficulty in looking at both? If you need psychological research to convince you that the tactile signals of such an experience contribute to the elementary knowledge of two-ness, the evidence is there in how touch creates activity in the parietal lobe of our brain, the part that registers quantity. Even elementary holding has many sub schemas, as new dimensions are added, two-handed picking, eye–hand coordination, and hand transfer, all skills offering sensory knowledge not only about the properties of objects but also about the power to move and reorganise them.

- **Tracking**. At earliest levels tracking may be observed in fixing interest on particular items and following them. Scanning rows of objects is an important precursor to counting and the development of the internal image of a number line.

  The development of tracking or tracing activities continues to be of importance at higher levels, both in respect of pursuing information, and in making tactile memory imprints that support or compensate mental visual imagery. So the simplest forms of tracking schema are important first practice for more sophisticated tracking that we use in later life, for example developing the ability to make and remember letter or numeral forms, sequencing, following mazes or maps.

- **Alternating**. Being aware of more than one item and switching attention between them. The process of alternating gaze is a first step towards maintaining attention with more than one object, and that process must continue to grow, enabling us to learn to match and compare and develop all the skills that are based upon those fundamental operations. Just like the whole of computing power is built upon a myriad of yes/no decisions.

- **Pointing/itemising**. Noticing one thing at once and pointing and touching, are obvious precursors to counting. They involve not only the organisation of the child's own hands and digits but the coordination of looking. To extend pointing as a counting activity also entails developing 'alternating' schema, requiring the child to switch attention and maintain sequences of touching. Sequential touching provides powerful stimulus registering quantity in the parietal lobe.

- **Moving and transporting**. Children may move objects or collections of objects from one place to another. The processes may help them to make changes of quantity and experience conservation. Shifting items that have been pointed at one at a time, and combining a verbal note as each item is moved, are ways in which this schema relates to learning about counting.

- **Collecting/grouping**. Children might like to put things together, collect items in their arms or containers, connect and join. They may like to form and join groups of other children. Later they may like to create groups sorted by some kind of criteria. There are strong perceptual tendencies, such as similarity and proximity (see Chapter 6, 'Perception') that affect our explorations of grouping and all these activities have obvious connections to understanding processes that increase quantities. At later stages children may use scrap materials arranged, glued or fastened into lines; pieces of wood might be nailed into long connecting constructions. Strings, rope, wool are used to tie objects together. Sometimes children's drawings and paintings show a series of linked parts, with obvious connection to developing the understanding of number lines.

- **Separating**. Children may like to take things apart and separate items, observing a decrease to nothing. They may like to give things away, or enjoy activities where groups decrease. They may group by separating items. Such processes may illustrate practical subtraction or division. Eventually children need to come to an understanding that separating is the inverse of collecting, and eventually that subtraction is the inverse of addition.

- **Ordering**. A child may like making lines of objects; as with tracking, it is a precursor to counting. They may like being beside, in front, or behind others, joining lines of children. Later they may produce paintings and drawings with ordered lines or dabs; collages or constructions with items of scrap carefully glued in sequence. At more advanced stages they may place blocks, vehicles or animals in lines and begin to show interest in 'largest' or 'smallest' or sorting lines according to some criteria.

- **Positioning**. Children may like to place themselves in different places and positions, which helps them experience that there are different viewpoints. A child may be interested in placing objects in particular positions, for example on top of something, around the edge, behind. Paintings and drawings also often show evidence of this. Positioning has obvious connections with understanding space, but some positioning schema may include hiding and finding, which helps with growing an awareness of object permanence.

- **Orientation**. Children have interest in different viewpoints, as when a child enjoys turning round, finding a viewpoint, hangs upside down or turns objects upside down.

- **Dabbing**. A schema used in paintings haphazardly or systematically to form patterns or to represent, for example, eyes, animals in a field. An interesting schema giving powerful individual impulses associated with increasing quantities of marks. Some dabbing may be used to create patterns related to recognising quantities through the processes of subitising.

- **Dynamic vertical and horizontal schema**. A child may show evidence of particular interest by actions such as climbing, stepping-up and lying down flat. Feeling vertical and horizontal structures, such as poles, rails, or planes such as tabletops or walls. These schemas may also be seen in constructions, collages, or graphically in scribble, drawing or painting. After schemas of horizontality and verticality have been explored separately the two are often used in conjunction to form crosses or grids. These are very often system- atically explored on paper and interest is shown in everyday objects such as a cooling tray, grills, nets or boxes.

- **Trajectory**. An interest with things travelling or flying through the air – balls, planes, rockets, Frisbees – whatever thing can be thrown. May be expressed through child's own body movements, as large arm or leg movements, kicking, punching.

- **Diagonals**. Usually later than the vertical/horizontal schemas. Can be seen in the construction of ramps, slides. Drawings begin to contain diagonal lines forming roofs, triangles, and zigzags.

- **Enclosure**. A child may build enclosures with building blocks, boxes. Sometimes they are named as objects, buses, houses, fields, and things or people put in them, but sometimes left empty. In graphic form an enclosing line is often used to frame drawings when children are exploring this schema; sometimes they fill the enclosure or leave it empty. Enclosure is related to drawing shapes and collection or demarcation of sets.

- **Enveloping**. As an extension of enclosing children may wrap things up or put them in boxes with covers or lids, wrap themselves or others in a blanket or hide in boxes. Paintings are sometimes completely covered over with a single colour wash. Enveloping explores concepts of object permanence, constancy and conservation. It can be used to challenge memory and promote the use of imagery as a memory tool.

- **Circles**. Circular motions and manipulations are with the child from the very beginning, and later include rolling, spinning, turning, etc., which relate to positioning and orientation schema. Circles appear in drawings and paintings as heads, bodies, eyes, ears, hands, feet, etc. They are also used in representing animals, flowers, wheels, the sun and a wide variety of other things. They are also related to concepts of enclosure and part of the processes of representing sets.

- **Semi-circularity.** Semi-circles may be used in pictures or constructions to represent parts of bodies and other things. Mouths, eyebrows, ears, rainbows and umbrellas are a few of the uses for this schema, as well as parts of letters or numerals.
- **Radial**. Radiating strokes are used to represent suns, fingers, eyelashes, hair. Circle games provide experiences of looking towards different points of the surrounding environment, building concepts of directionality.
- **Rotation**. There may be a fascination with turning or spinning, A child may become absorbed by things which turn – taps, wheels, keys. They may roll pencils, Plasticine, cylinders along, or roll themselves. They may rotate their arms, or construct objects with rotating parts.
- **One to one correspondence**. Building upon other schema such as pointing and grouping children may begin to relate to the rules of one to one correspondence. They may like to match items to people, collect single items in containers, find partners to work with. There is often evidence of this schema in scrap collages and constructions where a child for example places single items inside each cup of an egg box.
- **Transformations**. Children may be interested in transformations of materials; they may experiment with changes in shape, volume, etc., working with practical materials, building up knowledge that may contribute to understanding conservation, for example, that mass, volume, quantity does not change unless something is added or taken away.
- **Functional dependency**. Although causal relationships are not fully appreciated, interest may be seen in the dependency of one function upon another, for example, pretending to turn an ignition key 'so that the engine will start'. The mathematical dimensions of this schema include understanding that something must instigate change, or that when events happen there are consequences, for example, quantities may change. These are fundamental appreciations that children must have if they are to realise that a problem can occur and can be solved – that rules apply, not magic.

*Schemas – forms of thought and signs of progress*

The schemas I have described are often very evident as we watch children's physical activities. The importance they have in providing practice supporting physical development is clear. In this chapter I have however been at pains to illustrate their important internal mental dimensions – how schema are 'forms of thought'. They provide the child with important learning information through all the sensibilities, but they make particular use of our senses of touch, movement and position (the *tactile, proprioceptive,* and *vestibular channels*) that we often neglect in our classroom fixation on visual and auditory communication. Schemas are forms of thought; they are parts of our conceptual understandings; not parts we can easily express in words, but nevertheless sometimes even more powerful or more exact than words in the way they prepare us and connect our actions to our kinaesthetic understanding of space, weight and quantities. That said, schema can also involve language and communication. What children say when they are playing, or during the processes of manipulations and mark making, often reveals their thinking. Equally, adults can contribute to their children's experience of related language by offering incidental comment as children explore.

I have discussed schema as means of learning, though we might also find them useful indicators of progress. Observations might show more sophisticated schemes or combinations being adopted as children progress. There may be some benefit in recognising that different levels of schema could be used to add detail when structures like P scales do not seem to have enough stages to illustrate fine points of progress.

*The achievements of the sensory motor learning*

This chapter has reviewed how learning that typically occurs in the first two years of children's lives is usually characterised by the coordination of sensory and physical skills that enable the child to satisfy the will to explore his or her world. Piaget described this era and gave us the notion of a sensory motor stage of learning. We have also seen that while children are developing those physical skills they are also developing related mental ideas, and that their cognitive understanding develops through their physical and sensory activities. During this stage of their lives their ideas are still dominated by their perceptions and they are unable to form abstract concepts by generalising their ideas. Sensory motor intelligence is limited to real actions, performed on real objects; it is interested in practical immediate outcomes, but this is a situation which will begin to change

As children progress, gathering concepts through their sensory motor exploration, they also begin to communicate actively about the world around them. They like to test and provoke that world and they discover that their actions have effects. As we saw in Figure 10.1, during the later stages of the sensory motor period they begin to understand that they can communicate about cause and effect, they learn that they can share attention. The nature of this realisation is of enormous importance to the child's ability to learn and it is a process that is refined during the next phase of learning, when children refine their thinking and communication skills.

# 11 Becoming aware of thinking and understanding about things

When children widen their horizons beyond the personal exploration of their own bodies and immediate sensory environment, they become social learners. It is a time when they develop representational intelligence; they become interested in communicating and thinking, about quantities, space and time. The processes of communication extend their exploration beyond the boundaries of their immediate selves and personal environment. They begin to use the concepts and elementary language of maths for social purposes, which enables them to learn so much more about their world. Although the learning that we will look at now usually occurs between the ages of two to six years, a period that Piaget describes as pre-operational, and extends into a period of 'concrete operations' that typically spans the primary years, for children with learning difficulties aspects of the issues we discuss may begin later and continue into their adult lives.

## Beginning to make concepts

Following but overlapping with their period of sensory motor learning, children begin to connect experiences to make and represent ideas. At first the connections are simple formed from direct associations, for example all men are called Daddy. Later they become more discerning, drawing together ideas from experiences, or deducing from them to create more sophisticated ideas.

During this time children still learn a great deal through doing things with real objects. At first they are mostly concerned with internalising imitations and actions. As far as children are concerned at this stage, what they see is what they've got; their understanding is still dominated by their immediate perceptions, and their thinking is intuitive rather than logical. But it is during this time when children really work on developing the ability make mental representations, memorisations that enable them to think about things symbolically, thus extending the range of their thinking and communication beyond the immediate present and opening the possibility of thinking about things that are not present – the beginning of abstract and logical thinking.

There are a number of key abilities and concepts that relate to moving beyond the perceptual here and now that are important during this period. Understanding changes and conservation, sharing attention, understanding that other people can 'think', and being able to represent things symbolically, are all important contributors to children's abilities to form concepts, communicate and learn. Once again, though all these aspects of learning are abilities that we often take for granted, they are very important for pupils with special needs. Taking a look at some of these aspects will illuminate considerations we need to make about the nature of the maths curriculum for children who are learning to communicate and learn through real experiences.

### What I see, is how it is! – conservation

Piaget considered that at this stage children have a tendency to make judgements based on what they see, and this could lead them to be misled by perceptual tendencies. For example, for a five year old a quantity of juice that she thought was too much when presented in a tall thin glass could seem acceptable if it was transferred into a wider glass and therefore looked like less. The child is perceptually deceived, as we discussed in Chapter 6, because she centres her thoughts only on the height dimension and thinks the quantity must have changed because the shape has. She lacks the concept of conservation – the principle that, unless something is added or taken away, quantity remains the same. These effects that Piaget thought lasted until the child was six or seven undoubtedly do occur, and learning about the conservation of quantities and number are important phases in the child's development. However there is a great deal of evidence that the rudiments of conservation can be found in children at earlier ages, when problems are couched in ways that the children understand (Donaldson 1979). So although their concepts of conservation may not be mature or able to be expressed abstractly children may have a practical sense of conservation, which we can build on, earlier than Piaget thought.

For our very special pupils, difficulties with sensory organisation and perception will make it even more difficult to gather and apply the concepts of conservation of number and quantity. So the beginnings of a mathematics curriculum for them should include experiences that illustrate both constancies and how things change. For these pupils we need to provide experience, and use language to illustrate many practical examples of conservation of quantity, volume, weight, etc., so that they can broaden their experience and tune in to the application of the concepts in different circumstances, promoting horizontal progression by widening the contexts of understanding which they may over time generalise in what for most is a gradual spiral to the next level.

## Becoming aware about understanding

### Sharing attention

Fundamental learning entails exploration but unstructured experiences may not necessarily advance effective learning. So without unduly eroding the important benefits of exploration, teaching strategies must guide the focus of learning by suitably shaping and ordering materials and experiences, giving children a better chance of seeing the point. In order to plan teaching we need to be aware of what children already understand. Equally, if children are to gain the intended learning they need to share our awareness on the focus of learning. For example, if we were using a group of toy cars, with the objective that the child might practise itemising them as part of the processes of learning to count, the desired learning would not even be pursued if the child's attention was wrapped up in the colours of the cars. So we need to be able to share attention to learning experiences, and we cannot take it for granted that we are sharing attention to the same features.

*Points of view*

## Childhood egocentricism

From his observations Piaget concluded that typical children in the two to six age range are absorbed in their own perceptions, consequently they are not able to understand that another person has a different point of view. He described them as 'egocentric', or to put it another way they think that we all see the world in the same way as they do. Practical examples of the effect might be that a three year old hiding under the table thinks that because she cannot see someone's eyes they cannot see her, while the four year old who blocks your view of the TV doesn't realise you can not see the same as he sees. This explains why children insist on speaking to you while you are on the phone and are so surprised when you are annoyed. They are not entirely selfish, but their thoughts are 'centred' on their own perceptions, and to be able to appreciate another person's point of view they have to learn to 'de-centre' their thoughts, so that they can move their mind's eye from one point of view to another.

Incidentally, at this stage children find it easier to follow positive instructions like 'hold the budgie gently' rather than negative ones such as 'don't squeeze the budgie!'. Parents who have no appreciation of these aspects of egocentrism may tend to think of their children as junior adults and be full of frustration when they perceive their children as wilful beings, who interrupt conversations, disobey commands, stand in the way, and treat budgies badly.

The concept of childhood egocentricism was a strong influence in Piaget's theories of how children's minds develop, but he did not get it entirely right. There is no doubt that children's thinking is often self-centred but we might also observe in them behaviour that shows us that they are not entirely egocentric. For example, they are able to give instructions to help people who are blindfolded, or they will hold pictures up with the face away from themselves for viewers to see (Gelman 1979, Siegel and Hodkin 1982). Piaget had based his experiments on asking children what they thought could be seen from different points on a model mountain. It seems the children found the questions confusing, because the experiences were not real to their experience (they were disembedded). In different experiments when the questions were asked in terms that they understood because the problems related to events that were really in the scope of their experience (embedded), children showed they were quite able to envisage a different person's view. Margaret Donaldson and her colleagues (1978) demonstrated quite conclusively that children do have the ability to de-centre at a much earlier age than Piaget realised – showing us that while it may not be fully developed, the ability to take another person's point of view is not entirely absent in the pre-operational stage, indeed it is definitely developing.

## Adults and egocentricism

Egocentricism is not something that completely goes away as we become sophisticated adults. We all have plenty of examples of misunderstandings that occur when we make assumptions about what other people know. In her book, *Children's Minds*, Margaret Donaldson relates a Laurie Lee story about his first day at school. When the teacher asked him to wait for a while by telling him to 'Sit here for the present', he waited expectantly all day for a gift. While the child was naive, it was also true that the teacher simply assumed that he understood her direction for him to wait for the time being. In fact Donaldson makes the point that, as an adult, the better you understand something the more risk there is of behaving egocentrically, expecting other people to understand you. This we might readily appreciate when we ask for street directions in a strange town, or when a computer whiz tries to explain the workings of software to us, or, dare I say it, when the maths teacher explains long division. So we do not completely grow out of egocentric tendencies – there are many circumstances when we are well aware of the need to establish, in our own minds, what other people understand, in their minds, and in such cases we are able to de-centre. In other circumstances we may remain oblivious of misunderstanding. The reason that this discussion about egocentrism is important to us is because it is about how we come to understand each other.

### Learning to appreciate other people's thoughts

The ability to understand another person's point of view is achieved and refined through experience; normally we simply assume that children achieve such skills. We have, however, already seen that even adults are prone to get the wrong idea, and if we are to be effective teachers we need to ensure that we appreciate possibilities of mutual confusion. We may need to be even more aware of possible misunderstandings when we are communicating with children who have communication or learning difficulties, because they may be at early stages of communication competence and not be so tuned in to ways of recognising that they do not understand what we are asking them to do, and may not have ways of asking for clarification.

What are the experiences that help us appreciate what other people are thinking? We saw in our earlier consideration of sensory motor learning (including Figure 10.1) that the journey of learning through sensory and physical exploration involves the child in encounters with cause and effect, and that children typically begin to enjoy communicating about these things with others – sharing attention and communication about changes. Such interactive exchanges introduce children to new ideas about the functions of language. Initially very young infants use sounds and gestures to express their most basic needs and desires – hunger cries and satisfied gurgles and coos. Their idea is that language gets them what they need, or enables them to express their basic feelings. Kathryn Nelson (1973) described nonverbal, and later verbal, language that fulfilled such purposes as 'expressive', and this is the first language function that children use – it is centred only on their own expressive needs. In contrast, when children begin to share attention with other people about objects and events they encounter language that is responsive, that refers to and describes things. Nelson called this kind of language 'referential'; it is the language of exploration, and ideas. When children share this kind of language with adults it naturally illustrates to them that other people have different perceptions and responses. To understand that another person has a different perspective on what you are both looking at, encourages the child's progress towards greater awareness of themselves and others. It illustrates that other people have ideas, and they can be shared. This is having a *Theory of Mind*, that is, realising that they, and others, are creatures, which think (Dunn 1988). This enables children to realise that other people 'know' and that they can learn from them. It is an essential understanding, which takes the child beyond learning that is based on sensory and physical exploration and confined to the real objects around them, and on into the world of ideas.

We cannot always assume that children who have special difficulties have this perspective, and therefore developing an awareness that they can communicate about quantities, changes, space and time, and learn from communicating with other people about what they see, is an important part of the foundations of the mathematics curriculum for them, and in our interactions we need to create and take opportunities to help them become receivers and users of 'referential' language and pursuers of shared experiences relating to quantifiable aspects and changes of the world around them.

*The mathematical value of another point of view*

Children who appreciate that another person has a different point of view are ready to extend their understanding of mathematics beyond the fundamental experiences of immediate personal exploration, which has taught them about physical properties. They are ready to communicate about quantities, space and time. Such communication will enable them to absorb the cultural heritage that will give them number words, to describe quantities, show them processes that result in being able to calculate and a myriad of other ideas that will help them define, describe, discuss and appreciate the world around them.

What can we learn from this that will help our teaching?

Referring to our earlier example, one poignant thought would be that young Laurie Lee's teacher was completely unaware of his confusion and probably never knew unless years later she read *Cider with Rosie*. Likewise Laurie sat there all day confused, and that is the nature of misunderstanding, it is often misunderstood! Piaget asked the wrong questions and got wrong answers, but he did not understand he was wrong. It is not just children who are egocentric, psychologists and teachers also fail to 'de-centre'. When we ask a question or pose a task can we be sure our pupils understand what they are supposed to do? Remember, the more you know, the harder it is to realise how little, or how differently, someone else may understand. So when we have tipped a tub of lovely bright coloured toys on the table and asked 'how many?', does Robert know that we really mean 'will you count them?' Since he may often hear the dinner ladies ask 'how many potatoes?, he might think we mean 'do you want?'. Or he might just be attracted by lovely colours and like to handle or sort them. There are many ways to misunderstand, even when you are good at language – when you are just piecing it together there are even more. Have you ever asked a child to count and then seen them keep their eyes on your face, as they try to point to the objects. What is going on? It could be a lot of things, but here is a theory. One way that children progress their language learning is by making the best sense they can out of what is said to them, and then keeping their eyes and ears open for feedback about their actions. Hughes and Grieve (1980) found that children tried to make best sense out of even bizarre questions. So the child has made a guess at what you want and is watching your face for clues about how they are doing. Imagine you are in a foreign land and you only know a few words of the language; the rapid streams of speech seem incomprehensible, but if you do think you hear one of the words that you know, you make a guess at what the speaker means, using every other clue that you can, what he has in his hand, what he looks at, how he smiles or frowns or points. Some of our children are in the same position, and we do not appreciate it, because we know so much about what we say and what we want.

The ambiguous way that mathematics uses ordinary language in special ways does not help. There are so many possible confusions, 'two' and 'too', 'add' and 'had', and if we talk about 'order' or 'take away' we might even conjure up a desire for a pizza or a chicken korma. Perhaps the most profound twist in all this was exhibited by Piaget and shared by children. He didn't understand that he didn't understand – it happens to us all. When we present learning experiences and materials, we need to have our antennae open for misunderstanding, including our own misconceptions. To make things clear we need to provide many physical as well as verbal clues, use eyes and pointing, use demonstrations and use many ways to highlight the desired outcome, including getting things wrong and highlighting the mistake. Though many of the children who have profound learning difficulties do not have the opportunity to stand in the way of the TV or frame awkward questions for us to deal with when we are already busy, the complexity of their learning difficulties may still be compounded by an egocentric view of the world, and our egocentric assumptions about them too. So the least we can do is to try to understand what they understand. Sharing attention to an event is one thing but are we both focusing on the same thing?

### Sharing attention to counting

The fact that we might not be focusing on the same things when we count together with children is supported by research into children's beliefs about counting, which has showed us that, despite being able to perform quite well, a high proportion of children do not understand the adult's purposes of counting before they start school (Munn 1997). Research showed that preschool children had ideas about counting as a social experience, they thought it was for pleasure, or to please others, but it was rare for such young children to explain that 'it was to know how many'. Their impression was that it was a social or playful activity but they did not connect it with quantification. Penny Munn could see a combination of things that alongside the preschool child's lack of appreciation of other people's mental activities might contribute to lacking understanding about why they were counting with an adult:

- During joint counting activities between very young children and adults the process of saying words seems important, but the actual aim of finding quantity is often not emphasised.
- The strength of children's own natural concentration on the physical aspects of counting activities, touching and handling, often obscures the adult's intended mental function of finding quantity.
- Children are dependent on adults to provide for them, they have no urgent real reason to check and tally, so counting is usually a game.
- Count words often occur as parts of games that are not to do with quantity – 'One, two, three – Go'.

If such typical preschool children have not yet seen the meaning beyond the social façade of the counting they do with adults, how do children with learning difficulties fare in the process? Is there any wonder they sometimes watch our faces, rather than the objects they are counting, to check they are making sense of what we asked them to do. If we could 'read' behind their eyes, what would be the question in their mind? 'Does he want me to touch them?', 'Shall I make that *too – three* noise?'

Penny Munn has a number of suggestions that might help us make our early counting and modelling activities more effective.

---

**Making modelling & teaching of counting more effective**

- We need to establish what children believe we are doing together when we count. We will see in our later review of how children learn to count that it has many subskills. We need to be able to see which of these things like itemising, ordering, naming are the things that they think we want them to do.
- Though we need to be aware when their counting is only a form of recitation that needs to develop, we also need to take their non-numerical counting seriously. Although Piaget believed that young children's counting activities were meaningless, he was wrong in the sense that their recitation of number words is important practice establishing word order. Their non-quantitive recitation of number words is also an important point of social contact we can share with them and from which we can help them establish connections with quantity.

- We need to make the purpose of counting explicit. She suggests that as we are involving them in the use of counting words we could also muse aloud, providing feedback about aspects of quantity that are involved. Children respond well to this kind of incidental information, and it is a feature of instructional TV programmes like *Sesame Street*, and even as adults we use forms of thinking aloud, to direct our actions. We will come back to this point about 'directive speech' in a few moments.
- We need to encourage children to use numerical goals, making use of counting for tallying, checking and comparing items and events that are real essentials in their lives and activities.

We have seen that both young children and adults need to be aware that other people have different mental processes, and that there is a tendency to assume other people have the same experience as ourselves. This tendency needs to be overcome if we are to communicate with each other. Children often both have a working practical knowledge of small quantities, and separately are able to produce a series of counting words. Because adults have knowledge of the purpose of counting, when they observe children exercise their early counting skills there is a tendency for them to think that children have also integrated these two aspects of counting. This is not always the case and when we are teaching children to count we need to be aware of ensuring that we emphasise the connection of the activities of itemising and recitation to the purpose of establishing quantities. These connections must be made if children are to count meaningfully or to understand in the processes of comparing by number, addition and subtraction.

### Speech and thinking

We have all observed children speaking to themselves as they play, and can often appreciate that some of this is like thinking aloud. Vygotsky, the great Russian psychologist, called this private speech, because a lot of it was something that children did for themselves, not intending it as communication with others. Vygotsky proposed that this thinking aloud was gradually internalised and became thinking (Vygotsky 1932). There may be room for some debate about the role and use of private speech in the learning of very special pupils, and such debate would have many angles. For example, pupils without expressive language may have no experience of it, while some autistic children may be fixated users. Though our discussion here must be limited, I feel that there are some ways in which knowing about aspects of private speech may be useful to our teaching and other ways in which it may be a thought-provoking phenomenon, that might help us understand our children more.

*Self-directive speech used to feedback and prompt*
Returning for a moment to the teacher's use of musing aloud, you might worry about muttering to yourself in the relatively public classroom, and you may feel the need to master this technique in a way that eludes the ridicule of your colleagues, who may be far too self-conscious to accept that something can be made of this idea. Nevertheless it is a powerful tool and akin to the technique of being 'in role' that drama teacher's use. In fact Shakespeare often used the verbal aside to ensure that audiences could follow the plot.

Vygotsky (1932) and his colleague Luria (1961) observed that children used some of their private speech in order to guide and direct themselves, and that gradually this speech was internalised. Despite the internalisation, and the age difference, most of us resort to directive speech occasionally, for example as we mutter the directions of a recipe, or follow instructions for setting the video. This directive function is quite natural to children and they have no problem in absorbing it from others as incidental feedback. If used as suggested by Penny Munn, it has the advantage of informing the child's thought and action processes without drawing the child into the many possible confusions of direct communication. Readers may remember my reference in Chapter 7 to creating non-demanding but informative monologue by 'speaking through objects', which was suggested as a useful approach by Donna Williams (1992), an autistic girl. Speaking alongside, providing indirect instruction or comment, may be a route for offering some guidance to such pupils.

Guiding speech is spoken as if you are thinking to yourself. It can be used to clarify the problem, suggest an approach, prompt the next answer, confirm a good action. The use of external speech to comment on events and your own actions is in a sense making thought concrete (hear-able). This is appropriate during the pre-operational period when children are still learning a great deal through doing things with real objects, yet beginning to move towards using their memories of things, actions and events to form internal concepts. In their own development the use of directive speech is a stepping-stone to internal thinking; if we skilfully use it to feedback to and prompt them we are tuning in to and encouraging their thinking.

*Internalising speech*

Vygotsky proposed that children move from speaking aloud as they play, through a phase of muttering and on to internal thinking. The process of internalising speech shows that the child is becoming able to make internal verbal representations, that is, verbal ideas, which are abstracted from their generalised experiences. This is part and parcel of developing the child's ability to think symbolically. It is a process that children who have typical language skills do, so naturally, that we quickly assume that they both use verbal thinking and understand verbal instructions. We will see a little later that these assumptions may not be always wholly accurate.

Many children with severe learning difficulties have language development that is delayed, or disrupted, and for these pupils it could be useful to support their use of private and directive speech in order to promote the internalisation of language as thought. Examples of how this could be approached are providing feedback by musing, as described above, or by encouraging the children to talk their way through processes or events, visualising and verbally describing what they might expect or do next during their learning activities. This is similar to how advanced driving instructors ask drivers to give a running commentary as they drive, or athletics trainers ask athletes to visualise and relate the sequences of their performance. It is worth noting how techniques like this make links between the different forms of symbolisation, visualisation and verbalisation; connections might also be made to different sensory modes.

Many pupils with profound learning difficulties have disrupted expressive language skills and will not have had the usual experience of either the concrete processes of directive speech, or the hours of private speech dialogue that young children experience as they play. Neither will they have benefited from the gradual processes of internalising their own speech, but that may not mean they have not internalised any symbols. Many such students clearly do have receptive language, they respond to our interactions and can obviously remember and anticipate things and events. In some circumstances they may find it useful for another person to run through the commentary, or speak through objects for them.

It seems obvious that, for us, all learning involves an interplay using different kinds of symbols and representations at a variety of levels. If we are to enhance learning opportunities for pupils with communication or sensory difficulties for example, we must consider the nature of that interplay, think about what kinds of internal representations they make, and how and what kinds of symbols they use. Indeed thinking about the nature of symbols is useful in relation to understanding any person's learning.

If we are asked to express our thoughts we are usually expected to express them in words. This leads us to assume that thinking is primarily verbal. But let us refer back to Einstein who described his first mathematical feelings as 'Initially involving visual and muscular processes', only later being translated into the symbolisms of words or numbers, inferring that there was a deeper and perhaps fundamental layer of thinking. We might also remember the evidence that we have seen from neurologists who have shown that our early concepts of number develop from visual or even auditory recognition of numerosity, and that we construct an internal number line that people describe visually. In Chapter 12 we will see that young children can do addition in their heads just as long as they do not have to rely on formal mathematical symbolism and thinking. All these considerations encourage us to think that there are some fundamentals that underlie verbal or numerical symbolic thinking, and perhaps it is important for us to help develop these fundamentals especially in the learning processes of pupils who have special difficulties with language.

## Thinking symbolically

Piaget proposed that infants and young children were unable to think symbolically. Judy DeLoache (1987) demonstrated this was the case with very young children when she used a model of her room, in which she hid a miniature teddy behind the model sofa. She found that two-year-old children could remember where to find the hidden miniature in the model, but were unable to use the model as a reference to find the real teddy. However children of only three years old were able to locate the real teddy. This demonstrated that they had moved on to being able to connect between objects that were used as symbols and the real things. It suggested that providing the children understood the task, and the symbols were meaningful to them, they were capable of using some forms of symbolic thinking at a much earlier age than Piaget had suggested. This process of coming to understand that one thing can represent another is an important concept in simply understanding what a number is. At a different level it is also an understanding that underpins algebra. So while we may appear to be discussing a very early childhood skill, at different levels our discussion may also be pertinent to the ways that some of our students may address Attainment Target 2 Number and Algebra of the National Curriculum (see Chapter 13).

Recognising the representation of things with objects, pictures or images are early stages of appreciating visual or tactile symbolism, which extends through relating finger counting and other tallies or mark making, towards developing an understanding of the symbolic nature of numbers. Indeed the very act of giving a quantity a verbal name such as one, two or three, is in effect representing it symbolically. It therefore seems reasonable to suggest that learning about the occurrence and use of all these kinds of symbols will be an important part of learning about how quantities relate to numbers, while children are in this phase of 'pre-operational' learning.

*Symbolic representation*

Children with severe learning difficulties often have difficulty with the translation of symbolic representations such as learning to read. On the other hand, symbol systems like Objects of reference, Makaton, Rebus and PECS, are often supportive, offering prompts that help them separate and make sense of the information flow by highlighting the most important features within particular statements, instructions, etc. Tactile, visual and auditory symbols can help children form mental representations of quantities, in their respective sensory modes. It may be worth noting that as well as identifying visual groups, the infants in Karen Young's experiments (see Chapter 8) could discriminate between different groups of sound beats, and equate sound groups to visual groups.

## Sensory symbols of number

In the process of helping children establish concepts of quantity and connect quantities to number names, we may find it useful to use sensory symbols for them, to see, hear, handle and feel through movement. Children may be helped to strengthen symbolic connections between number names and their own internal sense of number if sound patterns and movements are used to represent or reinforce their visual or tactile experience of particular quantities. Small consistent collections that they can feel – tally sticks, strings or tally bags (for example two large marbles in a small net bag such as you get free with washing powder) – can be used as symbolic tokens to represent or mark events.

In our western culture we underestimate the use of smell and taste which are much more important and finely tuned in African and Asian cultures. Given some of our pupils' propensity to mouth, sniff and taste and choose, there might be some ingenious ways of symbolising or reinforcing other symbols and sequences, using children's olfactory or gustatory channels, to mark a sensory distinction of a sequence of events. I am sure Flo Longhorn would get in here, including such activities within her numerate cookery (Longhorn 2000).

*Symbols supporting counting*

Symbolic representation becomes a vital part of the language of mathematics, and as with reading, working with numerals often presents difficulties for SLD pupils. An overview of strategies children use to keep track during counting, and aid the making of comparisons, may illustrate how some forms of symbolism may help our special pupils, and stimulate our thinking about how to include remembering, recording, scoring, computation and comparison within learning activities and teaching strategies.

## Body parts

Body parts have been used as means of representing quantities, counting and even calculation since pre history. The roots of number systems in all cultures lie in the use of body parts, particularly hands, as means of representing, remembering and calculating quantities (Dehaene 1999). In Chapter 8 we noted the unique and powerful roles of index finger pointing and coordinated sound making, for denoting individual entities, both as a precursor for the development of joint attention and communication, and in highlighting or confirming a sense of one-ness (Butterworth, G. 1998).

We have noted earlier the powerful sense of 'one' that comes from holding a single item in one palm, and how different it is when both hands are occupied. Three is too many to hold, and is therefore a beginning of the concept of 'many'. We have also seen earlier that children have an inner sense of those small quantities. To move towards extending that sense into numeracy, they need to experience the appropriate number names, connecting them to the quantities that they sense, and develop the resulting ideas about sequence and 'order' so that they create a fundamental internal number line. Some of our pupils may be at the level of understanding 'one' or 'one more', 'two' 'three' or 'many'. These pupils are likely to have physical or sensory difficulties that profoundly disrupt learning. In our search to find alternative channels we should associate our use of number words, or sound making that marks out sequences, with touching or holding, giving them strong tactile or kinaesthetic associations, through hands, feet, ears, eyes, elbows, knees. The parts and symmetry of our body have been an influence on the development of our understanding of quantity since the origins of our species; such powerful personal symbols should not be left neglected.

**Finger counting**
It seems certain that historically finger counting preceded counting with special words. Linguists tell us that the origins of number names are rooted in the words for fingers and hands. All this relates to the unique and direct connection described earlier in the book between the area of the brain that both controls the fingers and deals with spatial orientation, the left parietal lobe; neurologists have found that it is also the area of the brain where numbers are represented (though not numerosities). Both Butterworth, B. (1999) and Dehaene (1999), in their separate books, discuss these relationships and suggest that counting on the fingers is an integral part of the process of developing and extending the mental number line on which we represent quantities. It is certainly true that if we observe typical infants and children as they are developing their numeracy skills they spend hours manipulating their fingers and looking at configurations and combination of fingers muttering number words. During these processes they begin to remember and understand the relationships of numerosities in terms of visual and tactile sensations of finger patterns. They do all this naturally, because unlike in the early Christian days of the Venerable Bede we do not teach finger counting now, although the uneducated child street traders of Brazil are adept and very accurate.

If body parts have connections to quantity, beginning through our senses of one-ness and symmetry, we might regard fingers as extending that role to be the first symbols of counting. Though actual strategies differ, the purposes for which children use their fingers in counting seem to be common to all cultures.

- The single finger points and so denotes the individuality of one item.
- Fingers are very useful in that they can be both objects to count and symbols of counting (Hughes 1986).
- Children keep tally with fingers during a count, using them as symbols to represent objects, or to represent events, that occur and then are gone. So they are not only concrete referents but also enable us to make a record of the abstract, providing a useful visual and tactile aid to memory.
- They are useful as calculating tools in representing the parts of simple arithmetic problems, but are also available to represent the processes by being manipulated.
- Using fingers may be seen as a symbolic development beyond itemising objects. Their use extends the processes of pointing and touching that are important parts of itemisation.

All that we have discussed here relates to the processes of mental representation that begins during the sensory motor learning period and illustrates that, although for convenience I have described them in separate phases, sensory motor learning and the dawning of symbolic representation are inextricably overlapped and intertwined.

Children who seem unaware of these processes or those who are unable to manipulate their own fingers are disadvantaged in experiencing these sensations that provide important foundations for understanding quantity. It may be helpful for them if teachers use touch as a communication medium as they count, so that the children are provided with tactile/spatial signals about quantity, at the same time as they are offered visual or auditory numerical information, symbols or language.

### 'Written' symbols

Children's written representations of number begin through the processes of scribble. Through interaction with adults they begin to realise that marks can be meaningful. At first it may be difficult to interpret meaning in children's marks, but after scribble they progress towards written representation of number and pass through a further three stages, Pictorial, Iconic and Symbolic. These are illustrated in Figure 11.1. The first two relate strongly to the one to one principle.

- *Pictographic representations* – Where objects being counted are drawn depicting some of their characteristics as well as the numerosity.
- *Iconic representations* – Where simple marks are used to tally or represent the objects. Despite being quite abstract, iconic representations are used even by preschool children. Hughes (1986) was surprised by the proportion of preschoolers that used iconic representation. He accounted for its frequent use because of its similarity to finger counting and its appropriateness for keeping track of events.

**Idiosyncratic**
Children's earliest notation responses may look like random marks, though children may consider them to be meaningful. At first they may be at the level of simply beginning to realise that making marks is meaningful. Later they may begin to try to correspond marks to quantities they try to represent.

**Pictographs**
Pictographs use one to one representation. They represent some elements of the items. They may not necessarily be as pictorial as the example I have shown but may include similarities like shape, colour or position. Pictographs can be positioned to create order.

**Iconic representations**
Iconic representations make a specific mark for each item being represented on a one to one basis. Though they seem to be quite abstract they are used quite early even by preschool children, perhaps because they easily relate to finger counting and are useful for cumulative processes, marking turns and keeping tally on events. Icons are often placed in an orderly way.

**Symbolic numerals**
Typically developing across a period from three to seven years. At first they may be poorly formed, gradually more mature numerals are developed followed by writing number words.

**Figure 11.1** Children's written number symbols

- *Symbolic representations* – May at first be distinctive but personal markings, but with the progression of writing control they become conventional numerals, and later words.

The relationship between pictorial representation and making a mental visualisation of a quantity can easily be understood, and how it might help as a memory strategy, or provide visible evidence for the child to work on, will also be clear.

The use that children make of their fingers is apparent to any observer and the development of keeping tally by making iconic marks can be seen as a step extending finger counting. Both provide a mode of symbolisation which helps the child retain focus, firstly on accounting for whether an object is there or not, and secondly as a cumulative record which helps memory and can be worked on later, if calculation is required. Pictorial and iconic recording also help children keep track of quantities and provide concrete visual records for them. It may be useful to encourage children to use mark making or tally keeping to support counting activities and events. It seems likely that they need to be fully grasped before the relationships between quantity and more symbolic numerals can be realised; the use of numerals may normally begin during the pre-conceptual stage, or around the time children prepare to start school, but its mature use will stretch over a number of years into the period of concrete operations. We will see further evidence of how fingers and symbolisations help children learn when we look more closely at the development of counting in the following chapter.

# 12 Working on real things – the beginnings of numeracy

We have seen how between the ages of two and six years children usually work on and learn from real things and practical events; in the process they also learn about learning. They become able to understand that they can communicate about quantities, time and space; they become aware of the social interactions of learning and start to make and use internal representations that enable them to communicate and think about things.

## Concrete operations

Typically between the ages of six or seven and on to around eleven years children generalise about explorations and experiences to develop concepts. They step towards the start of abstract thinking, because the generalisations take them beyond the immediate here and now. But at the beginning their ability to abstract is not fully formed, because their judgements may still be dominated by direct perceptions, so their thinking is intuitive rather than logical. For example, if a Plasticine ball is rolled out to form a sausage they may think it becomes more, because it is longer. We discussed the issue of conservation in the previous chapter, and it continues to be an issue into this phase that Piaget described as a time of Concrete Operations. At the beginning of this stage children may think logically but only about concrete events, maybe grasping concrete analogies. They are still dependent on learning from real things. During this time their powers of logic gradually succeed the dominance of their perceptions, and they extend the use they can make of symbolic thinking and move towards maturing abstract thought.

For typical children the period of concrete operations spans the primary years, though for pupils with special needs it may remain a constituent part of their thinking into adulthood. During the early part of this period of learning children are typically beginning to develop their understanding of numeracy, including the fundamental development of counting and early calculation. These are the earliest stages of learning described in the National Numeracy Strategy and are covered in the Reception and Year 1 teaching programmes. Some children with profound learning difficulties may not have developed the fundamental skills to access these levels of learning, and others with severe learning difficulties may still be working at such levels for many years. To provide an appropriate curriculum for them we need to look in greater detail at what the fundamental learning that leads to understanding about quantities, counting and understanding changes and calculation entails.

## Counting

As easy as one, two, three! we take counting for granted – like reading, it is one of life's basic skills. Like talking and thinking, most people seem to assume that the skill of 'counting' just happens. Those of us who work with children who have severe learning difficulties are very aware that this is not the case.

Generally teachers of young children are very conscious of subskills that children need to learn before they read. Pre-reading activities are well understood and a wide range of materials is commercially available to help develop constituent skills for reading. Most maths schemes on the other hand give only cursory acknowledgement to the constituent skills of learning to count and they move very quickly to using counting as a tool for mathematical and arithmetic processes. Though there is research information available that looks at how children learn to count there is less practical guidance for teachers that illustrates how children learn the skill, or provides material to promote the constituent parts of 'counting'.

### The parts of counting

An obvious manifestation of counting happens as children learn to speak and use sounds that relate to quantity. Delighted adults begin to use rhymes, stories and songs to teach them the number names, and are soon rewarded by children repeating them. Proud parents relate that they can count to three, later ten, and so on. There is however much more to counting than repeating sounds. In fact it involves doing many things at once like rubbing your tummy and patting your head or in the more precise language of the psychologist:

> When counting the child must co-ordinate the production of two continuous active sequences, saying the number words and producing points, while concurrently co-ordinating the points with a set of spatially distributed objects. These requirements, accurate production of number words, plus their co-ordination in time with pointing and in space with objects allows considerable scope for error. (McEvoy 1989)

But even that is not the end of it, because all this word production and itemising needs to be done with a purpose and as we have already noted young children are not always aware that the purpose of the counting is to ascertain quantity (Munn 1997). Furthermore, these purposes require us to understand some principles of counting.

Though there has previously been very little explicit description of the parts of counting in our curriculum documents, including it would make an important contribution to the mathematical development of special pupils. If teachers know about the parts and principles of counting, they will realise the interplay of constituent skills, and appreciate the nature of learning opportunities necessary for those who have difficulty with the learning. By considering the parts of counting we can find suggestions about:

- which parts of everyday activities to emphasise so that children become aware of what counting is for and about;
- appropriate skills to practise;
- relevant levels of content for differentiated activities within the numeracy hour;
- relevant learning objectives to be included within the P levels, or other structures that we use to set our pupils targets (see Chapter 13).

## Knowing the number names

Though Piaget (1965) identified that children's recitation of number sequences and facts were mathematically meaningless, later researchers suggest that such recitation is useful rehearsal. It establishes the sequence of words and prepares a framework that children relate to as they develop other counting skills.

### The initial acquisition of number names

Though they may use number names referring to small quantities at an earlier age, children usually begin to acquire the verbal sequence of number names around the age of two (Fuson *et al.* 1982). In their daily experience they hear and imitate the sequence in rhymes, song, etc., and as adults count for them. Evidence about how children acquire words from the context of their use suggests that initially they may not perceive the sequence as separate words, but as a relatively meaningless string of rhythmic sound.

### One-two-threefourfiveonceIcaughtafishalive

Nevertheless this is a phase of acquisition, and their learning is assisted by the continuity and rhythm of the sound sequences, which cue and prompt sound recall, and help to fix the order of sounds. This process is culturally well understood and is part of the repertoire of interaction with infant children enjoyed by mothers and fathers the world over. It is also recognised and included within Foundation and Reception stages of our curriculum documents. Separating the sound flow into separate words and establishing the order of those words comes as a later phase of elaboration.

Children who have learning difficulties progress more slowly, and a paradox occurs, because nursery rhymes are inappropriate to their chronological age: so we refrain from these kind of activities, and yet they still need the vital support given to memory by clues of rhythm and intonation. There is a challenge to find or create adaptations of popular songs, football chants or raps, that can supply this kind of support to their learning. Sound pattern clues are also lost when the children's physical difficulties slow down the processes of counting activities and there is a need for us to provide supportive feedback through gesture and intonation to maintain sound clues.

### Elaborating the list of number names

Hearing and observing adults using number words, children may recognise that they are being used to describe quantities, and through repeated experiences they recognise that specific words relate to specific equivalent quantities. A further part of the elaboration phase occurs when children begin to use those words as number names and the words become 'objects of thought', that symbolise quantity. The words become useful for meaningful counting when the child:

- Realises that each word has its own meaning and acts as a name (*noun*) for a specific quantity.
- Connects each word to their internal representations of quantity, and its place on their mental number line.

When this knowledge is absorbed the child will begin to recognise that there is a fixed order on which they can progress up and down; they will become able to say number names onwards or backwards from a given point. The elaboration process begins with the smallest numbers and stages of acquisition and elaboration overlap.

**Some processes that children need to focus on as they learn number words**

**1. Acquisition**

Learning the sequence connected in a stream, of rhythmic sound.

Beginning to separate the individual words, maintaining their order.

**2. Elaboration**

Confirming the connection of individual words to a related quantity.

- Using words as adjectives to describe quantities.

- Using words as nouns to describe **any** occurrence of specific quantities.

Connecting words to their own internal representations of its quantity.

Confirming the order of occurrence, connecting words to their internal number line.

- Knowing the order backwards.

- Knowing the sequence onwards or backwards, from a given point.

**Figure 12.1**   Learning the words of counting sequences and connecting to meaning

For example, 1 2 3 may become firmly established, while later numbers are only verbal. The reliability of order and quantity is gradually developed.

*Larger numbers*

Some pupils with severe learning difficulties progress to using numbers beyond ten. The ability to use larger numbers develops through a similar pattern of acquisition and elaboration and as with smaller numbers, different aspects of number sequences – teen structure 11 to 20 and the decade structure 20 to 90 – may be being learned at the same time but be in different phases of acquisition, e.g. when one to ten has moved into the phase of elaboration, the teens may just be starting to be acquired as a sound sequence. Even with typical children the whole process takes a number of years and the rate at which children develop the skills is varied.

The process depends upon children coming to understand rules by which the number words are combined. The language we use presents obstacles. Far Eastern languages follow a more logical progression, because 11 is expressed *one ten one*, 12 is *one ten two*, or 23 is *two ten three*, etc. European languages do not reflect base ten structures so purely; we have special words that need to be learned for the teen numbers and to mark decades, all of which create additional load on memory. For example, the words eleven and twelve have no connection with previous count words, and the remainder of the teen words and decade words like twenty are a little obtuse. Spare a thought for the French who even have to cope with remnants of a base twenty counting system where 84 is *four twenties four*.

When children who have learning difficulties reach the stage of learning the teen and decade structures it is especially important that we should illustrate to them that it is not something completely separate, by ensuring that numbers are strongly related to their base ten roots.

Counting objects

We have already seen that counting involves more than the recitation of number words, and we have discussed some of the underlying understandings about quantity that exist in children's number sense and need to be developed. Children extend this understanding by connecting visual and tactile learning with the verbal symbols of the count words, and later the visual symbols of numerals. So tactile activities are important aspects of the parts of counting.

In order to count a group of objects children must be able to itemise them and tag each with a number name (Schaffer *et al.* 1974), and we have already discussed the significance of pointing and the neural connections between fingers and the mental construction of our number line. Providing no mistakes are made tactile itemising provides a strong link connecting the verbal count with the child's internal representation. Itemising involves pointing, and linking the word to the object as they point. In order to do this accurately they must:

- pay attention to the objects;
- control the motor activity – pointing;
- make verbal output;
- coordinate these actions in both space and time;
- remember which items have been counted and which are left to count, which is called Partitioning.

It is easy for them to make a mistake while:

- controlling the physical act of pointing and controlling their attention to space;
- timing saying the number words at the right moment as they point.

For young children touching is an important part of this process of itemisation, and provides a physical prompt to help with timing the saying of the naming word. Remember, it also sends signals to the brain's parietal lobe areas responsible for relating quantities and spatial concepts and so connects to our mental number line.

---

**Teaching needs to help children overcome these easy mistakes that they make when counting**

- Fail to correspond pointing to individual objects.
- Fail to correspond the sound with the pointing action.
- Miss an object.
- Itemise an object more than once.
- Miss a number name.
- Apply the same name twice.
- Confuse the order of names.
- Lose track of what has been counted and what remains to be counted.
- Don't stop the verbal sequence at the last object, keeping on because of the rhythm.
- Don't realise the last number is cardinal.
- Miss some objects because they don't think they should be included in the count because of their colour, shape, position, etc.

---

**Figure 12.2** Mistakes that children make when counting

Martin Hughes (1986) notes how children still resort to pointing and tapping to assist their counting even when objects are out of sight. He also reminds us of the powerful use made of finger counting all over the world as a means of assisting both itemisation and partitioning, illustrating the importance of tactile and motor activities within counting strategies, and, therefore, the importance of providing activities that involve touching or pointing skills and rhythmic tactics such as finger counting and tapping when we teach children who have difficulties, especially as they eventually move from physical partitioning to practising mental partitioning.

### Five counting principles

As they coordinate physical pointing and oral naming, to count accurately there are a number of rules that children need to apply. Gelman and Gallistel (1978) described five principles necessary for accurate counting. The first three principles relate to 'How to Count' and the last two are about applying counting. As you read through these principles you will soon see specific things that children need to practise, or others that lead to misconceptions. Even typical children suffer these misconceptions but usually overcome them by experience: for special children they can be entrenched and we need to clear them up by explicit teaching. But first we need to see them and sometimes the simple things are the hardest to see.

*How to count principles*
**The one to one principle**
**Understanding and ensuring that each item receives one tag only**. This requires:

- Physically keeping track or mentally *partitioning* – which items have already been counted and which remain.
- It also requires *tagging* – summoning up and applying distinct names one at a time.
- It is necessary to realise that the nametags are specially for counting with, they are nothing to do with other characteristics of the items being counted.

In the early stages of learning to count children may be vague or imprecise about their pointing: they wave their fingers in the general direction, but let the rhythm of the oral counting sequence dominate the speed at which they count, and consequently lose correspondence. Later they become more aware of the importance of coordinating the itemising and tagging, and they develop strategies such as touching or moving items, for keeping track, and noticing if they have double counted or missed items (Gelman and Meck 1983).

There are many times when working or playing together we can make sure good tally marking or itemising takes place. There are many different levels of itemising, vocalising and naming. All too often in games, etc., we simply expect the child to count successfully. This is a prime area for breaking skills down; games provide motivating opportunities to practise the parts of counting.

**The Stable Order principle**
**The nametags must always be used in a stable order**. Using number names to provide ordinal names for things being counted presents the child with the problem of remembering a long list. Bearing in mind the general limitations of short-term memory (Miller 1956) – the human mind only being able to keep track on around seven plus or minus two items at once – in our teaching we need to recognise the valuable role of intonation and rhythm in offering connections and prompts that

make it easier to create memorable 'chunks' or connections of information, and so help learning a stable number sequence.

**The Cardinal principle**
**The final number represents the size of the set**. When the child understands this principle they recognise that earlier numbers were temporary steps towards the last number tag, which is special, because it is the cardinal number and represents 'how many' items have been counted. Appreciating the importance of *cardinality* is an important milestone in a child's mathematical development; it is a keynote in understanding that the process of counting has a meaningful and useful purpose.

Fully grasping the cardinal principle depends on understanding the previous two principles; it therefore matures after them. There are four phases in its development (Fuson and Hall 1983).

- Reciting the last number with no clear idea that it relates to quantity, but because they realise it is the response the adult expects.
- Understanding that the last number of the count relates to the quantity.
- Understanding the progressive nature of cardinality, i.e. if they are stopped in the middle of a count they can say how many they have counted so far, then carry on.
- It is necessary for a child to grasp the cardinal principle before they will be able to compare magnitude represented by numbers, or understand that the next number in a sequence represents a larger quantity, or use the technique of counting on to determine or compare the equivalence of groups. (The implications of this point are also discussed by McEvoy 1989.)

We can emphasise the special importance of the last item in a count by intonation, but we also need to make sure children realise that counting is not just sound making; its purpose is to find out 'how many'.

*The principles about what can be counted and applying counting*
**The Abstraction principle**
**Counting can be applied to any collection – real or imagined**. Adults realise that they may count physical or non-physical entities, similar and dissimilar things, objects that are not present, or even ideas. Young children on the other hand count physically present items and they group things in accordance with how they see their immediate relationships.

Variations in material properties or position may affect their view as to whether an item should be included in a count. What children of different ages or stages of development conceive as allowable within a counting sequence raises important considerations.

- What they might think about including or leaving out of the count on grounds of physical properties, position, etc.
- Are they able to understand they can count objects they cannot see?
- Can they count events as they happen, and events that occur elsewhere?
- Can they count ideas?

**The Order Irrelevance principle**
**The order in which items are counted is irrelevant; the same cardinal value will be reached**. This principle requires knowledge about the previous four principles. Grasping it entails understanding that:

- Each counted item is still a thing, not a 'one' or 'two', etc., because number name tags are temporarily given for the purpose of counting, not renaming things, and they do not necessarily adhere to the objects once the counting is finished.
- Whatever order the objects are counted in the same cardinal result occurs.

It is necessary to grasp this principle in order to be able to generalise the use of counting as a tool. It helps us confirm the consistency of the quantity of a group and it is confidence in that consistency that enables us to be sure about making comparisons. Such confidence helps us to override the messages of perception that may confuse us when spatial changes make things appear bigger, and it may therefore underlie our ability to recognise the conservation of number.

*The potentially confusing language of mathematics*
Without giving it a thought we use number names in different ways:

- They are 'Ordinal' when they are used as labels to represent a place in an order, e.g. 6 on a ticket means the sixth seat in the row. When used in a counting sequence ordinals are temporary tags.
- They are 'Cardinal' when they are used as labels to represent quantity, e.g. 'six' on the packet means it contains six biscuits.
- Sometimes numbers are just names, 'Nominal', with no direct connection to quantity, e.g. telephone numbers.

We even interchange this usage without warning as we count. Pointing at each item in turn we say the number names in order, 'one, two, three', as if they were the names of the things we were pointing at, but reaching the last item we change our attitude. One and two seem to become irrelevant, three is of cardinal importance, as we ask the key question 'how many?' The recognition of this distinction between two ways of using the same words is fundamental in the development of thinking about counting. In order to make use of counting children must appreciate they are using the sequence of ordinals to find the cardinal value. But they must also realise that the cardinal is only a temporary label, that adjusts if things change. To add to the difficulty, sometimes numbers are just used as names, nominal; for example, if you were waiting for a number 52 bus you would have a very long wait if you allowed fifty-one buses to pass. The different ways in which we use number names may mystify children as they try to deduce the meanings of the words they hear or the processes they observe.

There is also another angle on this problem. Many of the words we use mathematically are the same or similar to non-mathematical words. Won, too, free, and for, may seem silly examples, because they are just sound alikes for numbers, but there are many more examples of translation difficulties when we suddenly change from speaking English and start to speak 'Mathematic'. For example, words like weight/wait, place, pair/pear, add/had, take, order, answer, away, on, unit, record, many, straight, right, round, are commonly used elsewhere with different meanings.

## Approaching the teaching of counting

### The first strand of the Numeracy Strategy
Now we have seen the complexity of counting, how its parts include physical coordination, mental and verbal skills, and learning rules, we might appreciate that when children have learning difficulties it might be beneficial to focus their learning

on targets that are parts within the skill of counting, and the focus we make for each child will need to depend upon

- how well they can carry out the physical and verbal operations of counting;
- how well they grasp the 'principles of counting'.

*The principles make a framework for teaching*
The five principles all work together and knowledge of them gives us a framework that helps us see the detail of children's mistakes or misconceptions. Knowledge of the specific parts of the counting process helps us to focus on the different needs of children who have different levels of knowledge and skills. When children have multiple difficulties they may be at the earliest stages, learning to communicate with us about single items; the framework helps us understand that they still need strategies for pointing, itemising, showing sequences, etc., and so prompts us to look for different ways of offering experiences of quantities, and alternative avenues of exploration and communication for them. We might use sounds, fluorescent items, or reinforce our use of a number name by touching fingers or tapping their wrist, or we may present items that represent specific quantities in number bags, e.g. two balls in a mesh bag, so that they can hold and feel two without the experience being disrupted by losing one. Items for counting can be linked on a string, or a knotted rope can be used to tally.

In practical teaching circumstances awareness helps us to accommodate the needs of individuals as they participate together each at their own level, e.g. Stephen may be only at the level of pointing to itemise, while Shafiq might be including word order, while Ruth might be able to track events on her fingers or score card. Together they can play a game of chance with an adult who calls on each for participation at the appropriate level, keeping the flow going with a skilful use of support, prompts and cues. Armed with consciousness about the detail of counting processes the teacher will be able to maximise many opportunities within everyday situations, develop events or games when there is opportunity to tally, match, visualise, compare, name, etc. Knowledge of detail will enable teachers to set the child realistic challenges, or offer support to ensure that the child learns from the process rather than fails by not being able to coordinate all the parts to produce the right answer. Figure 12.3 lists just some things that would occur in practical situations or games and could contribute to learning to count, which is an important constituent part of the first strand of the Numeracy Strategy.

## The beginnings of arithmetic

A conventional view of curriculum is one of linear and vertical progression, because preparation for each more complex skill is dependent on mastery of the previous. We teach skills in a specific order. When children progress quickly this gives a useful general view of the mainstream of learning. However, when children experience barriers that slow their learning we need to pay attention to meanders, and undertow. It takes time, and many repetitions in various circumstances, for learning to be generalised. Children need wide practical experience applying learning in many contexts.

A rigid view of vertical progress might lead us to suppose that teaching addition and subtraction would follow learning to count, and formally this tends to be the case in maths schemes. However, were we to follow this logic we would be unlikely to progress beyond trying to teach many pupils with severe learning difficulties to count, and we might not approach the practical uses of numbers that are useful to

| Counting principles | Activities that relate to the principles |
|---|---|
| **How to count** | |
| The one to one principle | Looking, listening, responding, pointing, touching, itemising, tapping, finger counting, moving and placing items. Coordinating sound making, touching, etc. Keeping tally with tokens or marks. |
| The Stable Order principle | Number rhymes, chants, songs. Give and take with cues. Ordered boxes, drawers, etc. Practical counting. Tally sticks. Number ropes. Number lines. Linear games. |
| The Cardinal principle | Practical counting, intonation, start and stop. Checking progress. Give and take, including 'how many now?' Carry on. |
| **Applying counting** | |
| The Abstraction principle | Count mixed groups. Count, hide and count. Count sounds. Use fingers to count items or people that are elsewhere. |
| The Order Irrelevance principle | Recount jumbled groups. Count items taken out of order. |

**Figure 12.3**　Activities that contribute to learning the counting principles

their daily lives. However there is good rationale for including practical estimations and calculation in our special needs curriculum, even when children are still learning to count. We have seen that infants have surprising innate abilities in their number sense; long before they can count they appreciate and compare quantities, and have intuitive perception that addition increases and taking away decreases (Starkey *et al.* 1983). Well before they understand symbolic notation they naturally use their body parts for keeping tally, and supporting their own systems of counting small groups (Geary 1994). Typical children have practical informal mathematical abilities that they draw from experience of applying their number sense to real events, because they have both innate understandings of quantity, and a disposition towards using them in comparative (mathematical) thinking. There is a cross fertilisation between:

- the abilities of their instinctive number sense, e.g. subitising and tactile experiences that form their visualisation of the internal number line;
- practical experience where they encounter accumulation and decrease;
- the processes and results of their counting experiences.

Through these interactions children use their early concepts and abilities in parallel, each contributing their part to the refinement of the way that they are used together; for example, the number line supports counting, while counting extends the number line. Though people may assume that children do not learn to add or subtract until they can count, counting itself is a process of addition, and counting backwards is subtraction. At very fundamental, practical levels these skills are being encountered and learned together, and important factors in these processes are the tactile experiences and visualisations that extend number sense and contribute to establishing and extending the internal number line.

## Practical arithmetic

Sometimes however, though some of our special pupils cannot count for us, they are able to carry out practical tasks, and this echoes observations that suggest typical children can do mathematical tasks in practical senses long before they can express their understanding. This raises an interesting conundrum – do we say a child has a concept when they can apply it practically, or when they can express it using words or symbols.

Hughes (1986) describes the abilities of preschool children to add and subtract small groups when the words used in the question relate to real items. For example, They will respond correctly to 'What is two giraffes and one more?' yet be unable to relate to 'What is two and one more?' – they will wonder what the question means, and might respond 'one more what?'. The evidence shows that children are able to calculate if the problem, or the language in the problem, relates to real objects Hughes' experiments demonstrated that this applied even when the objects were not there in front of them. He suggests that children are able to use visualisation as a calculating tool when the language used gives them something to visualise.

He suggests that their inability to complete questions like 'What is two and two?' is because they are couched in the language of mathematics and they do not at this stage realise that they have to translate. The language of mathematics causes much confusion because it uses familiar words in different ways.

Question:          'What is the difference between 6 and 11?'
Child's answer:    'Six is curly.'

The insights that Hughes' work offers us are:

- children's concepts of mathematical operations have a practical basis;
- many difficulties children have with mathematical problems relate to translating between their concrete understanding and the language that is used for mathematical purposes.

If we take these insights on board we have a practical basis and justification for including fundamental learning about addition and subtraction, that is, the second strand of the numeracy strategy in the curriculum for our special pupils. Our pupils' natural interest in things that increase and decrease will lead them to make anticipations and estimations, which are the precursors of calculation. They may not be able to describe their learning, but some may use it practically.

*Addition – combining*
Children's understanding of addition and subtraction begins with practical experience through which they learn to appreciate and anticipate accumulation and depletion.

Children tend to see addition as change by joining. The first stages of appreciating addition involve drawing items together and combining groups. When working with very small groups addition and counting are intrinsically linked. The earliest foundations of learning addition may be appreciating 'one' and 'more than one'; it may include putting items held in each hand together accumulating more than you can hold, or drawing groups of things together on the table to make more, or combining the contents of containers. During these activities we can use the key vocabulary of combination and increase such as: put another, together, add to, make more, are there more. We can help children anticipate more and how many more, and we can encourage them to estimate.

81

At later stages when we have named quantities in containers we can tip the items from two containers into a drawer to create larger groups and name them. This first stage of formal addition is:

- **The union of two sets** – at first, children having already counted out each set, then count all the items again after combining them.
- **Counting on** – is the second stage, when children presented with two groups count on from the first set presented – regardless of size.
- **Counting on from the largest** – comes later when they are able to recognise which is the largest of the two groups.
- **Later still children may retrieve number facts from memory**, and with larger numbers, decomposing one or both quantities and using number facts to make it easier.

Typical children may naturally move through these stages, but pupils with special needs may need to experience activities that illustrate and model them. We can target the different stages to help us fix on strategies that we model for children as we work with them in practical circumstances and games.

*Subtraction – separating*

Subtraction is change by partitioning or separating. Just as we have a natural attraction to notice accumulation, we have an inborn interest in observing decreasing quantities; both these fascinations are part of our survival instincts. The foundation of learning about subtraction involves appreciating that as things are taken away from you the quantity you have dwindles to nothing, and there are many circumstances in games, explorations and life experiences in which the process can be highlighted by adults for children, for example, giving and taking, losing, eating and drinking, coming and going. Just as with addition, the early experience of decreasing quantities should be accompanied by the appropriate key vocabulary, this time the vocabulary of separation and decrease: take, away, less, fewer, left, finished, no more, gone, none, etc.

The first processes of subtraction are separating or partitioning and describing the process as 'taking away'. The first level is to

- **Separating a group, and counting the remainder is the first level.**
- **Counting back as objects are removed** – or folding fingers back – is a second level.

Subtraction is not always just simply taking away; questions of subtraction are often expressed in ways that involve confusing language. Here are some examples:

- **Comparisons** involve working out the difference between numbers and the language of comparison is particularly variable, e.g. which is more, bigger or greater – less, smaller, fewer? For children the concept of more is easier.
- **Complement of sets**. When questions occur in the form 'how many are not?', e.g. how many are not black? Unless they are very tuned in children tend to miss the negative aspect of the question.
- **The inverse of addition**. When questions occur such as 'what must be added to three to make five?', or 'how many *more* do you need to make . . .?'

When we use these forms of language we may not realise how much we mystify our pupils.

Approaching teaching about addition and subtraction

**The second strand of the Numeracy Strategy**
We noted that addition and subtraction are intrinsically intertwined with counting. The thread that connects them is the internal number line, which is extended from its small beginnings in number sense by experience of accumulation and counting. Connecting and comparing visualisations of objects to the mental number line is an important facet of children's early appreciation of increase and decrease, upon which addition and subtraction are built.

Children with profound learning difficulties may be at the very early stage of beginning to appreciate that things increase and decrease. For them a wide range of sensory encounters and experiences are relevant, supported by skilled adult communication drawing attention to aspects of changing quantity and encouraging response. From that point on teachers need to provide experiences that support a continuum of learning in which children are engaged in observing changes of quantity and developing practical anticipations, estimations and calculations. The themes of combining and separating often work together and provide the background for many processes of exploration and use of appropriate language. Games and life occurrences are motivating circumstances in which practical problems need to be interpreted and solved. They provide wonderful opportunities for the use of both social mathematics and language. Teachers applying a knowledge of counting principles can ensure they make the most of learning opportunities that occur in games – ordinal turns, the need to point and touch, collect, match, score, compare, name and describe, can all be milked for repetitive practice of language and skills.

A good theme for teaching practical arithmetic is collecting – children have a natural affinity to collect. They are motivated by acquisition and stimulated to keep track on their accumulations, and losses. At very early levels of learning children may simply be involved in giving and taking activities. Later on, making collections starts with the process of putting things into containers, an activity that children love. All sorts of containers can be used, often with interesting properties that can be attractive to our senses – wooden drawers, tins with lids, or cardboard tubes make good sounds. Items and containers can also be found that are age appropriate – football cards and collector wallets, make-up bags. Hiding and revealing things using containers seems to stimulate curiosity. Children want to know what's inside, and we can easily exploit that natural interest to begin mathematical learning by focusing on the 'how many?' question, and by adding or taking items away. Concealing and revealing processes can be used to promote children's visualisation, anticipation and estimation, refining their abilities to complete images and group items, and form ideas about wholeness, as described by Gestalt psychology.

As children progress in practical activities we may move towards abstraction via processes of recording using pictorial and iconic representations as described in Chapter 11. Children of different abilities may be involved in the same or similar activities: the different levels of objectives we set for them to learn would depend upon the individual levels of understanding and manipulating quantities; the extent to which they are dependent upon real things to help them visualise changes; and the extent to which we need to help them by illustrating or translating between their practical understanding to the language of mathematics.

# Part Four

# The mathematics curriculum

## 13 The mathematics curriculum for special pupils

### Access to the National Curriculum

It is important that the curriculum we provide covers relevant aspects of mathematics. For some children with very special needs relevant learning will entail learning about its most deep-seated foundations – levels before the experience, use and manipulation of numbers. Others will move on to the recognition of numbers and counting, some pupils will learn to use numbers in practical processes and calculation, though they will still learn these skills through very small steps.

In their earliest incarnations neither the National Curriculum for Mathematics, nor the National Numeracy Strategy reached deep enough to describe the fundamental levels of mathematical learning. Their descriptions did not begin at the beginning, but at the point that typical children were expected to be at when they started school. We have seen throughout this book that there is a lot of learning to be done before that point.

Developing a relevant maths curriculum for pupils with very special needs entails understanding that mathematics has many levels and they are explored in greater or lesser depth according to the needs of individuals (Banes 1999). Throughout this book I have described many levels that we take for granted but which special children may need support in developing. A curriculum describes the course of learning typically assuming that learning moves on to progressively more difficult skills, and the National Curriculum is written in this way like a ladder. But when children have severe learning difficulties the speed at which they climb that ladder may be impeded, and they may need to spend more time exploring and confirming ways of applying learning at each level. For this reason in their desire to ensure that the National Curriculum benefits all pupils, both the QCA (2001), in its guidelines for planning and assessing the curriculum for pupils with learning difficulties and the National Numeracy Strategy have come to endorse a range of perspectives on progression:

- **Vertical progression** – as pupils develop increasingly complex skills and conceptual understanding.
- **Lateral progression** – as pupils widen and consolidate their understanding of skills and concepts, applying them to different circumstances at the same level.

- **Maintenance of abilities** – is also recognised as an important focus for teachers working with very special children who may have complex temporary difficulties or regressive conditions.

The statutory inclusion statement in the National Curriculum 2000 and the QCA (2001) guidelines for planning teaching and assessing the curriculum for pupils with special needs plainly recognise the previous shortcomings of the curriculum and state that staff should interpret and modify programmes of study at each key stage to teach in ways that match and challenge pupils' abilities. In order to modify the curriculum we need to consider how our children make progress.

### Describing the nature of progress

Figure 13.1 illustrates how lateral learning may progress vertically as children spiral to the next plane. In the illustrated model the labels describing the early stages relate to 'Levels of Experience' or activity. These levels were described by Erica Brown (1996) and are now adopted in the new guidelines as a framework for recognising attainment below Level One. The framework relates to the nature of changes in pupils responses as they move from the earliest levels of learning, i.e. simply encountering experiences, towards becoming more active learners, through the following overlapping levels:

**Encounter – Awareness – Response – Engagement – Participation – Involvement – Achievement**

(*Readers who wish to relate these generic levels of experience to activities that connect to fundamental aspects of learning about mathematics will find some suggestions in the three tables 13.7 to 13.9 later in this chapter.*)

It is important to note that the Levels of Experience are not in themselves intended to be measures of vertical progress, they are intended to provide a framework which

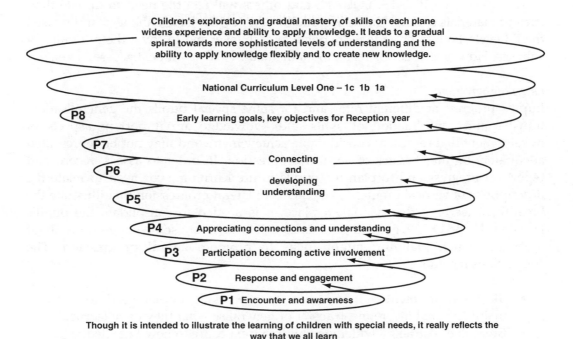

Figure 13.1 The spiral nature of progress

gives us insight into how pupils move through their learning processes. It is recognised that there may be complex factors that can temporarily or permanently affect pupils responses and these need to be taken into account. Assessing children's achievements in order to report on their progress or to plan for their future learning therefore needs to take account of both vertical and lateral dimensions.

## Measuring progress – P Levels and consolidation

### *Vertical progression*

Performance descriptions that have become known as P Levels have been developed in order to satisfy the need to describe vertical progress. The first introduction of the P Scales by the QCA (1998) as broad brush performance indicators for whole-school target setting in English, maths and PSE was a step forward, but there were shortcomings. They did not cover all curriculum subjects and they did not provide enough detail for assessing individual progress. Neither did they offer any guidance on subject content for the earliest levels of development, e.g. the most fundamental levels of mathematical experiences.

In their quest to find structures to help them to plan teaching and record individual pupil's progress schools and organisations have developed various assessment and recording systems. For example, Lancashire Education Authority enhanced P scales for recording progression with the PIVATS documents, which many schools have adopted to support recording children's progress in core subjects, and to analyse whole-school trends. Many other schools adopted EQUALS baselines and schemes of work, which cover all subject areas and are strong on developmental content. However they require a different scheme for SLD, PLD or MLD pupils and their strands differ from both the National Curriculum Programmes of Study and the strands of the Numeracy Strategy. These factors present dilemmas relating to duplication and continuity. EQUALS is well documented for its users so for the purpose of this book I will focus on appropriate interpretation of the National Curriculum and Numeracy Strategy, providing one curriculum for all pupils.

It is likely that PIVATS, EQUALS and others will feel the need to update their current materials because the new guidelines from QCA have enhanced and revised the P Levels, both to provide more detail at each level and to cover the full range of subjects. How new P Levels relate to mathematical skills will be discussed later.

### *Lateral progression*

Pupil's progress at different rates and for some special pupils the generalisation, transfer and consolidation of skills and knowledge are important aspects of development that represent considerable achievement, and may not be represented adequately on the P scales of vertical progression. In order to assess, record and report on progress and to plan for pupils future learning, staff need to relate the descriptions of vertical progress to elements of lateral progression that illustrate the breadth of learning that has taken place or is needed to consolidate the pupil's learning. In the QCA's general guidelines (2001) there are some suggestions about areas on which planning might focus to promote lateral progression. The suggestions include:

- **Skill development** – in addition to new skills pupils need to practise, maintain, combine, refine, transfer or generalise what they have learned.
- **Breadth of content** – widening children's exposure to new knowledge.
- **The range of contexts for learning** – challenging them to generalise and apply learning in new situations.

- **The variety of support equipment** – that enables pupils to take control of, affect and communicate about their environment.
- **The range of teaching methods** – e.g. offering different levels of support or challenges for independent learning.
- **Negotiated learning** – where pupils are encouraged to take a greater part in determining or organising their learning.

The diversity of opportunities for consolidating learning which we offer pupils is an important characteristic of their education that is needed to support vertical progression. Without consolidation specific vertical learning objectives may be sketchy isolated skills. Lateral experiences are therefore legitimate areas for target setting, both for individual pupils and for improving the quality of whole-school provision. It is important that we plan, record and target experiences that enrich and broaden pupil's mathematical skills by refining, generalising, combining or applying them in wider contexts, and that we describe the practices which broaden our curriculum. We should also recognise that personal development such as increasing independence or confidence, overcoming frustration or reducing behaviour that inhibits learning are all elements that occur across the curriculum and particularly in mathematics when there is an emphasis on social communication and practical activity.

*Reflecting the dimensions of learning*
The need to ensure that the way we deliver the curriculum includes consolidating experiences that support vertical progression implies that we need to be able to reflect both lateral and vertical dimensions in our assessment and recording. Vertical progression defined in curriculum documents like the P Levels lends itself to checklists, whereas the variety of lateral progression may require more descriptive facility. Recording systems need to facilitate both strands and yet be concise enough to be sustainable. ICT based systems like 'Numeracy Complete' produced by The Skills Factory offer such facilities as well as manipulation of data. Because of the diversity of special pupil's abilities when developing paper-based systems it is essential to try to reduce the bulk of material that has to be scanned to find relevant levels. A suggestion is that the recording document could be in the form of a recording bank, from which relevant pages covering the appropriate vertical levels can be selected for pupils individual files, and these could then be supplemented by additional evidence sheets on which teacher's notes about lateral experiences and achievements can be recorded, and targets outlined. Examples showing sheets that could be used for one strand of the Numeracy Strategy are provided in figs 13.2 to 13.4.

## Modifying the curriculum

The new National Curriculum 2000 now charges schools with the duty to modify programmes of study to provide suitable learning challenges, respond to pupils' diverse needs and overcome potential barriers to learning. So where we used to worry about a curriculum that did not fit our needs we are now empowered to modify it. The QCA have responded in 2001 by publishing new curriculum guidelines in all subjects for those pupils with very significant special needs who are unlikely to achieve NC Level 2 at Key Stage 4, most of these pupils will be working towards Level One for the majority of their school lives. In addition the National Numeracy Strategy will provide supplements of examples that will support appropriate interpretation of its teaching programmes to meet the needs of those

Pupil's Name........................................................... D.O.B. ...................

| NNS Strand 1 – THE NUMBER SYSTEM P1 to 3<br>Counting and recognising numbers. **Including appreciating quantity, noticing, itemising and remembering.**<br><br>**Contributes to YR Key Objectives and Early Learning Goals 1, 2, 3, 4** | Pupils Current<br>Key Stage<br>- - - - - - - - - - - - - - - -<br>**Assessment date** | | |
| --- | --- | --- | --- |
| **P1 OBJECTIVES**<br>Key levels of experience are *Encounter & Awareness – Moving towards response.* | Autumn | Spring | Summer |
| **P1 (i) To encounter experiences, examples are:**<br>• Encounter increasing and decreasing levels of stimulation or sequences of touch.<br>• Make brief sensory contact or interaction e.g. brief grasp on one object placed in the palm.<br>• Experience adults describing the object as 'One' and perhaps exchanging for another etc. | | | |
| **P1 (ii) To show emerging awareness, examples are:**<br>• Cooperate with physical modelling of rhythmic movement of limbs or manipulation of fingers and simultaneously attend to adult sound making.<br>• Use sight, hearing, smell, touch, to reach towards one object or respond to an event, anticipate the next movement, object or sound.<br>• Focus attention on well contrasted or distinct stimuli e.g. different groupings of fluorescent spots. | | | |
| **P2 OBJECTIVES**<br>Key levels of experience are *Responding, Engaging – beginning to participate.* | Autumn | Spring | Summer |
| **P2 (i) To respond consistently to familiar events, react to new experiences, examples are:**<br>• Maintain interest and attention to sensory input relating to quantities, e.g. maintain attention to sequence of events as adult count items onto their table.<br>• Maintains hold on single items, and takes it towards face for visual exploration or mouthing.<br>• Associates and anticipates sound making/number words with sequential activity, and makes sounds or other responses to accompany rhythmic limb or finger manipulations. | | | |
| **P2 (ii) Communicate preferences and responses begin to share participation, examples are:**<br>• Will reach to take items placed in front of them and collect them together on lap.<br>• Will choose the larger of two groups of desirable items when the difference is significant.<br>• Be encouraged to uncover hidden objects, and respond to sounds in the game sequence. | | | |
| **P3 OBJECTIVES**<br>Key levels of experience are *Participation, Involvement – beginning to gain skills and understanding.* | Autumn | Spring | Summer |
| **P3 (i) Show anticipation in familiar routines. Seek attention and request events, explore objects in more complex ways, observe the results of actions with interest, examples are:**<br>• Show anticipation in familiar number songs, or the next sound in a pattern, responding with varying vocal tones or with gestures in time with note counting.<br>• Show interest in sequential handling placing items in containers.<br>• Show anticipation/expectation in response to changing quantities in hiding and revealing games. | | | |
| **P3 (ii) Begin to use conventional communication, initiate interactions and activities, use gesture to respond to options, apply potential solutions systematically, examples are:**<br>• Initiate repitions of events, extending participation in sequences of gestures and sound.<br>• Following adult cue of a marking gesture or counting sound can touch or indicate 3 objects in turn.<br>• Appreciates the collection of scoring tokens in a game, imitates adult or peer gestures or sound making as they are checked by counting. | | | |

**Figure 13.2** P1 to 3

Pupil's Name............................................................. D.O.B. ...............

| NNS Strand 1 – THE NUMBER SYSTEM P4 to 8<br>Counting and recognising numbers. **Including appreciating quantity, noticing, itemising and remembering.**<br><br>**Contributes to YR Key Objectives and Early Learning Goals 1, 2, 3, 4** | Pupils Current<br>Key Stage<br><br>- - - - - - - - - - - -<br>**Assessment date** | | | | | |
|---|---|---|---|---|---|---|
| **P4 OBJECTIVES** | Autumn | | Spring | | Summer | |
| Follow others in number rhymes and songs and playing finger games. | | | | | | |
| Shows anticipation in pointing, touching and coordinates sounds using fairly consistent sounds as number words. | | | | | | |
| Copy an adult holding up fingers or picking up a number of objects (up to 3). | | | | | | |
| **P5 OBJECTIVES** | Autumn | | Spring | | Summer | |
| Vocally or using physical communication join in with familiar number rhymes, songs, stories and games. | | | | | | |
| Indicate one or two: for example using their fingers. | | | | | | |
| Recognise numerals 1 and 2, connect them to the words, know 2 is more. | | | | | | |
| Touch or point at two or three objects in turn applying a counting sound to each in turn. | | | | | | |
| **P6 OBJECTIVES** | Autumn | | Spring | | Summer | |
| Demonstrate an understanding of one to one correspondence, matching cups to places children will sit. | | | | | | |
| Use tokens or beads to record and remember quantities or make pictorial representations showing quantity of groups. | | | | | | |
| Join rote counting use numbers to five as 'ordinals' in familiar activities and games. | | | | | | |
| Count reliably up to three items, be able to make sets of three. | | | | | | |
| Has some recognition of numerals up to five, and realises numerals can record the number of objects. | | | | | | |
| **P7 OBJECTIVES** | Autumn | | Spring | | Summer | |
| Count reliably at least five objects. Understanding the cardinal. | | | | | | |
| Join in rote counting of numbers to ten and appreciate the use of numbers one to ten in games and real contexts. | | | | | | |
| Make tally marks to record a number counted. | | | | | | |
| Recognise numerals from 1–5. | | | | | | |
| Point to appropriate numbers on a number line. | | | | | | |
| **P8 OBJECTIVES** | Autumn | | Spring | | Summer | |
| Count reliably up to 10 objects. | | | | | | |
| Join in rote counting with numbers beyond ten. | | | | | | |
| Continue to rote count onwards from a given small number. | | | | | | |
| Begin to use ordinal number names – first, second etc. when describing position, or turn taking. | | | | | | |
| Compare two different quantities up to 10 saying which is more/less. | | | | | | |
| Begin to recognise numerals 0 to 10 and relate them to collections of objects. | | | | | | |
| Estimate a small number of objects and check by counting. | | | | | | |
| Start to record numerals to represent up to 5 objects with reversals or inaccuracies. | | | | | | |

**Figure 13.3** P4 to 8

Pupil's Name........................................................ D.O.B. ...................

## Record of Consolidating Experiences and Achievements
## Comments on Progress and Targets

This page may be printed on the back or inserted following each P level recording sheet or Yearly Teaching Programme checklist.

It is intended to accompany and provide supplementary information enhancing the assessment of vertical progress that is shown in P Levels.

This evidence of consolidating or lateral progress will also provide information for **Target Setting**. As the child progresses new sheets can be added to provide a continual record.

Comments are valuable to fill out our picture about the child's abilities and progress.

**Targets** – following assessment we should anticipate next steps and set new or revised targets.

| Assessment Date and Pupils current Key Stage | NNS Strand P Level or N. Curric. Level | Additional evidence or comments and Targets |
|---|---|---|
| | | Give information relating to: <br><br> • The effects of specific special needs, support or resources. <br> • Ways in which the pupil has widened his/her experience or ability. <br> • You may wish to note or refer to examples of pupils work. <br><br> **Target Setting.** Please highlight or underline targets and ensure that they are clearly dated. |
| | | |

**Figure 13.4**   Consolidating evidence

special pupils across the primary and secondary age ranges. The writers of the guidelines are careful to stress that they are intended to facilitate suitable access to the National Curriculum, they are not a separate or substitute curriculum for special pupils. Neither are they schemes of work, but they do suggest approaches to modification. They describe opportunities and activities through which children of all abilities can access suitable aspects of the Programmes of Study at each key stage in appropriate ways. The guidelines therefore provide a framework, which we can tailor to meet the needs of our schools. Ensuring that there is one source curriculum for all pupils and that schools can interpret it in ways that are appropriate to their lives and needs.

In addition to illustrating how work at particular stages might be open to interpretation at different levels the guidelines suggest a number of other ways that teachers may modify mathematics programmes of study to provide all pupils with appropriate learning challenges, these include:

- Choosing appropriate material from earlier key stages.

- Focusing on limited aspects of age related programmes of study that are specifically relevant.
- Using aspects of everyday experience that capture pupils attention and relate to aspects of mathematics which are important to their lives.
- Combining, consolidating, reinforcing or maintaining previous learning.

All of these approaches can sit well in mixed ability classrooms, when the National Numeracy Strategy long term planning framework is used alongside differentiation planned to allow pupils to draw different levels of learning from the same experience. The premise of the guidelines is that the programmes of study can be modified by interpreting the fundamental nature learning relevant within each section, e.g. the main focus for Number for some pupils will be to build upon their earliest perceptions of quantity. Such a premise is entirely consistent with the approaches to fundamental learning about mathematics that I have been outlining in this book and which is developed further in respect of the strands of the National Numeracy Strategy in the following section.

## The National Numeracy Strategy

The National Numeracy Strategy was introduced in 1999 and for mainstream schools it gave flesh to the National Curriculum, through its yearly teaching programmes and supplement of examples. It recommended a daily mathematics lesson in schools, and its frameworks set out coverage for each year group, by laying out suggestions for which aspects or 'topics' of maths might be taught each week, following a principle of visiting and revisiting aspects.

### The strands of the Numeracy Strategy

It is fair to say that prior to the implementation of the strategy dedicated maths lessons had been given a low priority in many schools for children with severe learning difficulties, most numeracy teaching taking place incidentally through cross curricular and life skills experiences. At first glance the strands of the Numeracy Strategy may seem to be framed for mathematics that is beyond the needs and abilities of students who have very special needs. However a thread that runs right through this book is the process of taking a microscope to learning and if we look very closely into the strands of the Numeracy Strategy, we can see how they relate to our pupils fundamental learning (Staves 2000). The interpretations listed below can be found as the top line of Figure 13.5, which shows strands of the numeracy strategy, and different levels of activity that children use as they work towards Level One of the National Curriculum. I would like to suggest that the strands equate in the following ways:

- **Strand one – counting, numbers and the number system** – is about perceiving and appreciating quantities, becoming aware of differences, comparisons, equivalencies, sequences, description and eventually about experiencing and using number names to signify quantities. Through these processes children acquire knowledge of quantity and skills of counting as everyday tools that help them anticipate, predict and manage their lives.

  Algebra is introduced at KS3 in the National Curriculum but has resonance across key stages because, it is about how one thing can represent another and involves seeing relationships and making connections, generalising them and realising that life has patterns and rules.

- **Strand two – adding, subtracting, and calculations** is about anticipating and appreciating changes that result in increase and decrease, moving on to manipulate quantities and represent the changes.
- **Strand three – solving problems** is about active responses, comparing, classifying and making things happen. Handling data, which is introduced at Year 3, is about putting information in order so that you can use it or think about it.
- **Strand four – measures, shape and space** is about experience, appreciation, and estimation and the practical measurement of all kinds of sizes, shapes, weights, volumes, time and the spaces we are in and around. It helps children appreciate and respond to similarities and differences of size, volume, weight, position, movement, duration and temperature. Children learn through trial and improvement, by exercising the processes of investigation and exploration on concrete experiences. They develop awareness and learn important aspects of the language of the practical world.

The interpretations are conducive to the suggestions in the QCA's guidelines about how special pupils can access the mathematics curriculum. While they relate to levels that are fundamental to mathematical learning that children usually explore before they start school they are also open to age appropriate application, through appropriate choice of learning activities. Figure 13.5 shows both the fundamental interpretations of the strands and how children's levels of response mature as they work up through the P Levels towards Level One of the National Curriculum.

*P Levels and the Numeracy Strategy*
We discussed earlier how the eight levels of the P Levels were designed to describe vertical progression towards NC Level 1. The National Numeracy Strategy has described examples of performance in each of its strands equating to the P Levels. Ann Berger and her colleagues (2000) also provided examples. An outline describing examples of the kinds of performance at each P Level from four to eight in each strand is also shown here in Figure 13.6. These descriptions provide a useful overview of the kinds of things we might expect pupils to do at any particular level. The descriptions are drawn up by associating how each strand of numeracy relates to the Performance Descriptions for Mathematics that are outlined in the QCA 2001 guidelines. Though they are not always very specific or objective statements, they are useful guides to our assessment of a pupil's level, because we can observe which descriptions best-fit a pupil's performance over time.

We have already noted that to give a true picture of a pupil's education experience we need to supplement our assessment of their vertical level with description of the breadth of their learning. Likewise we need to describe consolidating experiences and connect the levels of pupils' performance to practical aspects of learning, so that we can plan actual practical activities, that are age appropriate yet still include the kind of elements of fundamental mathematical learning discussed throughout this book. These include:

- Developing sensory, perceptual and attention skills, as they apply to experience of quantity space and time.
- Coordination of physical and cognitive skills related to the principles of quantity and counting and that enable their understanding and handling of shapes, space and measures.
- Promoting number sense and visualisation of quantities and changing quantities.

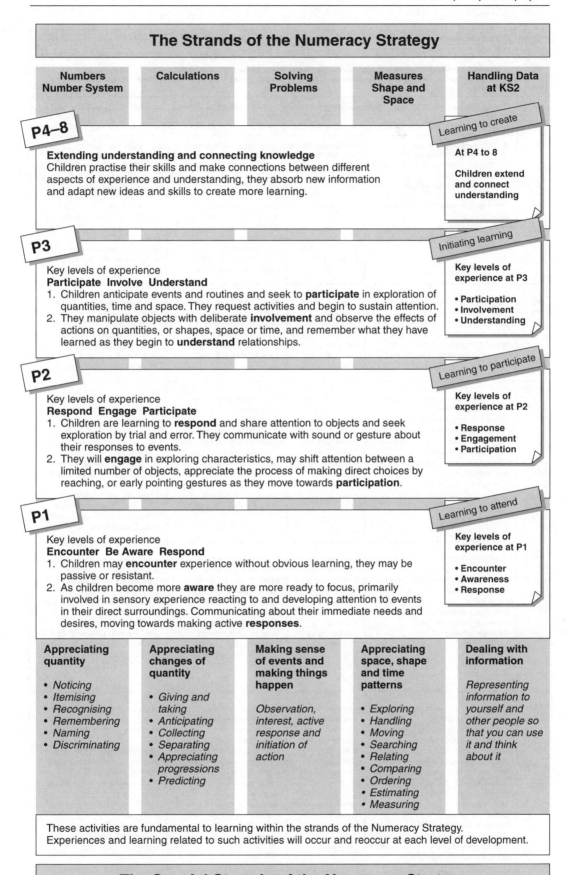

**The Strands of the Numeracy Strategy**

| Numbers Number System | Calculations | Solving Problems | Measures Shape and Space | Handling Data at KS2 |
|---|---|---|---|---|

**P4–8** — *Learning to create*

**Extending understanding and connecting knowledge**
Children practise their skills and make connections between different aspects of experience and understanding, they absorb new information and adapt new ideas and skills to create more learning.

At P4 to 8

Children extend and connect understanding

**P3** — *Initiating learning*

Key levels of experience
**Participate Involve Understand**
1. Children anticipate events and routines and seek to **participate** in exploration of quantities, time and space. They request activities and begin to sustain attention.
2. They manipulate objects with deliberate **involvement** and observe the effects of actions on quantities, or shapes, space or time, and remember what they have learned as they begin to **understand** relationships.

Key levels of experience at P3

• Participation
• Involvement
• Understanding

**P2** — *Learning to participate*

Key levels of experience
**Respond Engage Participate**
1. Children are learning to **respond** and share attention to objects and seek exploration by trial and error. They communicate with sound or gesture about their responses to events.
2. They will **engage** in exploring characteristics, may shift attention between a limited number of objects, appreciate the process of making direct choices by reaching, or early pointing gestures as they move towards **participation**.

Key levels of experience at P2

• Response
• Engagement
• Participation

**P1** — *Learning to attend*

Key levels of experience
**Encounter Be Aware Respond**
1. Children may **encounter** experience without obvious learning, they may be passive or resistant.
2. As children become more **aware** they are more ready to focus, primarily involved in sensory experience reacting to and developing attention to events in their direct surroundings. Communicating about their immediate needs and desires, moving towards making active **responses**.

Key levels of experience at P1

• Encounter
• Awareness
• Response

| Appreciating quantity | Appreciating changes of quantity | Making sense of events and making things happen | Appreciating space, shape and time patterns | Dealing with information |
|---|---|---|---|---|
| • *Noticing*<br>• *Itemising*<br>• *Recognising*<br>• *Remembering*<br>• *Naming*<br>• *Discriminating* | • *Giving and taking*<br>• *Anticipating*<br>• *Collecting*<br>• *Separating*<br>• *Appreciating progressions*<br>• *Predicting* | *Observation, interest, active response and initiation of action* | • *Exploring*<br>• *Handling*<br>• *Moving*<br>• *Searching*<br>• *Relating*<br>• *Comparing*<br>• *Ordering*<br>• *Estimating*<br>• *Measuring* | *Representing information to yourself and other people so that you can use it and think about it* |

These activities are fundamental to learning within the strands of the Numeracy Strategy. Experiences and learning related to such activities will occur and reoccur at each level of development.

**The Special Strands of the Numeracy Strategy**

**Figure 13.5** The strands of the Numeracy Strategy

| Level | Early Development<br>*See Figures 13.7 to 13.9 for more detail about the mathematical elements within Early Learning* | | | |
|---|---|---|---|---|
| P1 | 1. Pupils show reflex responses to sensory stimulation, **encounter** activities and experiences, may be passive or resistant.<br>2. Begin to show sensory **awareness** in relation to encounters and growing alertness to a range of people, objects and materials in everyday contexts. | | | |
| P2 | 1. Pupils show reactive **responses** that focus attention towards familiar people and objects, e.g. reaching, holding, turning to familiar voices.<br>2. They **engage** with others, make sounds or gestures to express simple needs or desires within the immediate environment. | | | |
| P3 | 1. They **participate** in exploring, showing anticipation and appropriate responses to familiar people, activities and routines.<br>2. They become **involved**, actively explore and manipulate objects, remember and apply potential solutions. They communicate choices, likes and dislikes using sounds, tones and/or gestures as they move towards gaining skills that will support understanding. | | | |

| Level | Numbers and number system | Calculation | Solving problems | Measure, shape, space |
|---|---|---|---|---|
| P4 | • Show an interest in number rhymes and games.<br>• Show anticipation when joining in pointing, touching and saying number names. | • Show interest when groups are combined or split, anticipate touching objects to count total. | • Show an awareness of cause and effect for familiar objects and activities.<br>• Look for object that has gone out of sight.<br>• Select similar object to match – e.g. pairing shoes. | • Show interest in difference in size, weight, space, etc., and appreciate that there are words to describe them.<br>• Begin to understand positions, stacking and aligning objects. |
| P5 | • Join in familiar number rhymes and songs, stories and games.<br>• Indicate One or Two, e.g. using fingers.<br>• Touch two or three objects in turn, applying counting sound to each.<br>• Realise numerals represent quantities. | • Compare small quantities.<br>• Cooperate with combining/ partitioning, responding to more or take. | • Match pictures or objects with help.<br>• Group or sort sets of objects by characteristics such as size or shape.<br>• Look for objects in their usual place. | • Compare one object with another according to its size or length.<br>• Manipulate positions: stacking objects, lining them up, putting them in and out of containers.<br>• Join in sorting shapes – be aware of names that describe them. |
| P6 | • Demonstrate an understanding of one to one correspondence.<br>• Count three objects reliably.<br>• Realise significance of last number name used when counting – cardinal.<br>• Understand more/fewer.<br>• Join in new number rhymes and games with assistance.<br>• Join rote counting to 5. | • With three objects demonstrate understanding, combining or partitioning by counting either total or remainder 2 + 1 or 3 – 1. | • Copy simple patterns or sequences.<br>• Sort objects, but not always consistently apply criterion.<br>• Make comparisons to solve problems – match items one to one to organise them.<br>• Use 1p coins shopping up to 5p.<br>• Search for things when they are not in their usual place. | • Understand words or signs that describe positions.<br>• Understand words about quantities, e.g. more, less.<br>• With support, compare two masses.<br>• Order objects according to size – be aware of words like larger, smaller, largest, etc.<br>• Participate with adult, making practical comparisons of more or less between large differences, weight, volume, etc. |
| P7 | • Count five objects reliably.<br>• Play games using numbers 1 to 5.<br>• Make tally marks to record counting.<br>• Begin to recognise numerals 1 to 5.<br>• Begin using language such as more or less, bigger or smaller, to compare – say which is more or less.<br>• Join rote counting to 10. | • Find one more and one less up to 5.<br>• With five objects demonstrate understanding, combining or partitioning by counting either total or remainder e.g., 2 + 3 or 5 – 2. | • Sort objects for a given criterion, e.g. all the silver coins.<br>• Talk about and attempt to recreate simple repeating patterns.<br>• Begin to use mathematical ideas about matching and sorting to solve practical problems, e.g. storing things in boxes. | • Use familiar words to describe position, size and quantity.<br>• Start to pick out particular shapes from a collection.<br>• Recognise directions forwards and backwards.<br>• Understand combinations of simple words to describe small quantities, size and position, etc., e.g. put biggest box at back. |
| P8 | • Continue the rote count on from a given small number.<br>• Count ten objects reliably.<br>• Compare two given numbers of objects, say which is more/less/fewer.<br>• Begin to use ordinal number names, first, second, etc., describing positions of objects or turn taking.<br>• Estimate small numbers of objects and check by counting.<br>• Begin to recognise numerals 0 to 10 and relate them to collections of objects.<br>• Start to record numerals to represent up to five objects with some inaccuracies.<br>• Join rote counting beyond 10. | • Find one more and one less than a given number of objects between 5 and 10.<br>• Combine or partition groups to 10.<br>• Use appropriate language, e.g. add, make, take, left.<br>• Respond to 'How many altogether?'. | • Recognise, describe and recreate simple patterns and sequences.<br>• Begin to use developing understanding of counting to solve problems encountered in play and practical circumstances.<br>• Begin to make simple estimates such as how many things will fit in a box.<br>• Sort coins in role play and give change. | • Make direct comparisons of two lengths or masses; find out practically which of two containers holds more.<br>• Show awareness of time through awareness of days of week and significant times of day.<br>• Use mathematical vocabulary such as straight, circle, larger, etc., to describe shape and size of shapes and solids.<br>• Use a variety of shapes to make and describe simple models, pictures and patterns. |

**Figure 13.6**   P levels for mathematics – abilities and activities leading towards Level One of the National Curriculum

- The development of communication and thinking skills.
- Relating their practical experience to representational, symbolic and abstract processes of the number system and fundamental estimation and calculation.

Though there is not space here to expand upon these processes some examples that give practical dimensions to the QCA descriptor for **P4 – Number: Show an interest in number activities and counting** might be:

- Copy holding up fingers in response to an adult modelling – perhaps as a response in a game of chance, reflecting the number pattern on the dice, or tallying items in a domestic activity.
- Indicate through sign, speech or gestures the next action in a number sequence, following a prompt, e.g. point at the fifth bottle of cola.
- Create sequences of sound or light patterns, that are regulated by counting.
- Working alongside other children in motivating events that give opportunity to, collect tally tokens, keep score and count, total and compare, e.g. bucket basketball shots. Resources: 1 bucket, 1 ball, magnetic tokens, magnetic whiteboard, marker pens.

Following the QCA guidelines (2001) the National Numeracy Strategy intends to produce supplements of examples that provide suggestions, that encourage suitable interpretation of its strands at primary and secondary levels.

### Subject content for the most fundamental levels

Readers will note that in Figure 13.6, P levels 1 to 3 still describe a range of performance seen in children's early encounters and responses to the environment. The descriptions given are generic to all early learning and do not illustrate how the child's activity relates to developing an understanding of a particular curriculum subject, so they do not have any content specific to mathematics.

There has been an ongoing debate about many issues relating to the lack of inclusiveness in this approach (Cavigoli and Reynolds 1999) and the new guidelines now include brief reference to subject focussed examples. While they may be useful to describe children's general level of development, the generic descriptions are not sufficient to give teachers' practical pointers to content or activities for subject lessons. Subject content guidance is particularly required when children are learning in mixed ability groups, and where teachers need to provide differentiated lessons to meet the inclusive needs of children together. In order to provide support for subject target setting the descriptions need to be enhanced to show how they relate to the distinctive content, distinct language and ways of thinking that characterise each subject (refer to Chapter 1). In relation to mathematics this requires descriptions of children's early interactions with quantity, space and time.

### Planning for very early learning

To give teachers a framework that will help clarify ideas about mathematical learning at P1 to P3 I have produced Figures 13.7 to 13.9 which suggest general outlines of the kinds of activities that children are involved in during their earliest stages of development, within each of the strands of the Numeracy Strategy. To help do this I have used three areas of teaching focus: sensory development, active physical development, sharing and communication. While these facets help to focus on ideas, in the actual process of learning they will usually occur simultaneously, it should be taken as read that where children have sensory difficulties teachers would seek alternative sensory channels. The grids are intended to support a next stage,

# Strands of the Numeracy Strategy

**QCA P1**
- 1. Pupils show reflex responses, they encounter a range of people, objects and materials in everyday contexts, they encounter a range of people, objects and materials in everyday7 contexts, may be passive or resistant.
- 2. Begin to show sensory awareness and focus briefly, with intermittent responses, e.g. brief gasp, or surprise at onset/close of interactions.

**EQUALS Level 1** • Reflexive reactions – Sensory awareness and responses.
• Reflexive reactions – Sensory awareness and focus briefly, with intermittent responses, e.g. brief gasp, or surprise at onset/close of interactions.

**Key levels of experience**
- Encounter
- Awareness
- Response

| Strand description • Reception • Y1 onwards | Counting and recognising numbers The number system | Adding and subtracting Calculations | Solving problems Handling data | Measures, shape and space |
|---|---|---|---|---|
| Interpretation that describes the strand appropriately for PLD pupils | Appreciating quantity. *Noticing, itemising, identifying, matching.* | Appreciating and anticipating changes that create increase and decrease. *Collecting, separating, Precursors to calculating.* | Active responses – making things happen. Organising responses, things and information. *Comparing and remembering. Precursors to recording.* | Appreciating and manipulating space, shape and time patterns. |
| *Teaching Focus* Sensory Development Including Attention and Perception | Learn to tolerate and enjoy stimulation. Use sight, touch, hearing or smell to encounter one or a number of objects or events. Extend glances and combine or coordinate with reflexive movements to improve coordination of attention. Feel sequential touching, and have assistance with rhythmic clapping of hands or movement of limbs. | Encounter and be aware of increasing and decreasing stimuli/ quantity: Light – brightness, flash frequency and rhythm, start, end, darkness. Sound – volume, timbre, rhythm. Quantity – sequence or increase/decrease of objects. Weight and volume – increase/ decrease. Touch – rhythmic pressure motion. Movement – frequency of stops and starts. | Encounter and respond to stimuli, begin to show response to different aspects of a stimulating event. Be encouraged to focus on main or particular features of a stimulus. Experience sequential events. See/experience objects being hidden and revealed. Have anticipation, surprise, pleasure or disappointment modelled. Visually track the movement of single objects. Glance between objects. | Encounter, be aware and respond to spaces, shapes, and time patterns. Hear associated language including intonation that emphasises description of size, frequency, etc. Encounter long and short periods of stimulus. Hear commentary or be assisted to feel changes during travel or movement, e.g. round corners or through doors in wheelchair. |
| Active Physical Development | Experience reaching towards and brief touch of single objects. Begin to combine reflexive movements to develop purposeful touch. Begin to extend glances at single objects and test with touch, eyes, nose and mouth. Have large and small movements, rhythmic movement of limbs and manipulation of fingers modelled physically. | Be helped to reach and touch and grasp objects, with single, both or alternate hands, experience assisted hand-to-hand transfer. Have objects taken from them and given to them. Experience finger manipulation and body part touching, associated with vocalisations about increasing and decreasing sequences. | Experience physical responses to their actions, e.g. give in response to their reach. Activities that encourage increasing control, extension and combination of reflex actions, e.g. modelling combined sweeping and grasping, or reaching and picking up, and placing items. Be assisted to pick up different objects and explore the nature of their different properties. | Extend grasping by modelling, feeling and holding of shapes and solids. Move or be moved in and through spaces of different kinds, e.g. open, narrow, low, etc. Experience people's responses to seeking and finding things. Remarks about things in usual places. Feel stretching and curling of body, limbs and digits. |
| Sharing and Communicating | Learn to respond and make sensory contact and eye contact with adult. Be encouraged to maintain focus on single objects. Hear language, with intonation that emphasises quantities, beginning and end of sequences, etc. See or feel gestures associated with quantities, including pointing, rhythm and counting sounds. | Be aware of comings and goings. Experience language intonation and gestures, associated with changes involving increasing and decreasing, or gaining and losing, having something or having nothing. | Encounter, be aware of or respond to communications in response to their own actions. Have comments that • Draw attention to objects and events • Encourage or indicate sharing – Do you like? Do you want? • Describe and question – Do you like? Do you want? • Praise anticipation, response, waiting. | Encounter, be aware of or respond to people's responses to objects, places, locations and events, changes in patterns or positions. Have their own vocal and physical responses to objects and events responded to by adults. |

*Most learning activities will include a variety of elements of focus*

**P1. Practical examples**
- Light and sound sequences may be used as stimuli for direct teaching. For example, an adult makes sound patterns by tapping or scratching rhythmically on a resonance board and watching for responses from the child laying on it, accompanying the patterns with language related to sequence. At earliest levels (P1.i) the child may show reflex response, even tolerance may be a significant achievement. Later (P 1.ii) the child will extend the level of awareness and begin to show an attentive response, perhaps showing some anticipation of the sequence continuing, or some desire for repeat.
- Haptic perception of weight, volume, shape etc. through touch or the development of the notion of 'Oneness' depends upon learning to hold items. To avoid tactile defensive responses items can be presented by stroking them along the childs arm towards the palm. Items like meditation chime balls create an additional attention stimulus that may encourage the child to look or listen towards what they are grasping. Language should describe the sequence of events, or the nature of one object then another. Later levels may include giving and taking.
- Child may enjoy inclusion in social interaction between adults and peers, e.g. as they respond to changes and sequences of a game, hearing the intonation of turn taking language of gaining and losing. Awareness of the differentiated learning taking place will allow staff to promote appropriate inclusion.

**Figure 13.7** Mathematical activities in focus at P1

## Strands of the Numeracy Strategy

| | Counting and recognising numbers  The number system | Adding and subtracting  Calculations | Solving problems  Handling data | Measures, shape and space |
|---|---|---|---|---|
| **Strand description** • Reception • Y1 onwards | | | | |
| **Interpretation that describes the strand appropriately for PLD pupils** | Appreciating quantity. *Noticing, itemising, identifying, matching.* | Appreciating and anticipating changes that create increase and decrease. *Collecting, separating. Precursors to calculating.* | Active responses – making things happen. Organising responses, things and information. *Comparing and remembering. Precursors to recording.* | Appreciating and manipulating space, shape and time patterns. |
| *Teaching Focus* **Sensory Development Including Attention and Perception** | Maintain interest and attention to sensory input relating to quantities. Look from one object/sound or light source to another. Show interest in difference between one and two items. Use visually directed reaching, or reach to sound of an object. Begin to use reach and point actions. | Engage in attention to changes of increase and decrease. Maintain attention and respond, showing awareness that change is occurring. Cultivate interest in object permanence. Feel objects that have been hidden as they watch. Encourage alternatives between one and two items, and encouraged to realise which is more. Subitising – encounter and show interest in small group patterns | Respond to stimuli and show an interest and desire to participate in changing, continuing or stopping events. Discern between different stimuli and signal like/dislike. Focus on specific features and maintain interest, cooperative exploration, repeat responses. Track visual sequences or arrays of objects. | Examine objects of different shape, size and length. React to spaces or shapes and show preferences about them. Show engagement in response to long and short time patterns or tactile experiences. Engage in attention to changing weights and pressure. Anticipate movements and destinations. |
| **Active Physical Development** | Apply more complex schema to the process of exploring objects, e.g. shaking, stroking and poking. Point, reach for, touch objects. Hold single items. Eye point from one object to another. Be assisted to experience hand transference or holding more than one object. Be encouraged to make sounds to accompany rhythmic limb or finger manipulations. | Gain and discard objects. Be encouraged to uncover objects that they have seen being hidden. Collect items together, on lap or table. Put items into and take them out of containers or bags. Touch fingers or body parts in turn. | Be assisted to actively participate in controlling and changing quantities or events. Holding, giving, moving, pushing, pulling. Use a two-handed scoop to pick up. Picking up and putting down. Be encouraged to control the placement, or position of items, or to choose to place things in different containers. Single switch control. | Move or be moved in and out of spaces. Reach and hold or otherwise engage in tactile experiences of shape, length and weight. Be assisted to make large exploratory movements feeling objects/ space. Notice things not in their usual place. Participate in response to instructions about stretching, curling, or reaching with body, limbs or digits. |
| **Sharing and Communicating** | Experience models of turn taking while attending to objects and quantities. Show or give objects to adults, be encouraged to alternate focus between objects. Hear language, intonation and see or feel gestures associated with quantities, including rhythm and counting sounds – have their own responses responded to. | Share responses to comings/goings and events, express an interest in frequency, increases and decreases. Express a desire for more or less. Show satisfaction and dissatisfaction, via facial expression, gesture, sound or pre-verbal vocalisation. Hear language, intonation and see or feel gestures associated with increase and decrease. | Respond to adult's comments and calls to look and then maintain attention to events. Initiate communication about changes using expression, gesture, sound or pre-verbal vocalisation. Make a response to immediate instructions. Seek recurrences of events. Hear and attend to language intonation, see or feel gestures associated with making things change. | Respond to adult's comments about spaces, shapes, length, weight, time, etc. and maintain attention to events. Initiate communication with expression, gesture, sound or pre-verbal vocalisation, expressing responses to spaces, shapes, etc. Hear language intonation and see or feel gestures associated with spaces, shapes, length, weight, time, etc. |

Most learning activities will include a variety of elements of focus

Figure 13.8   Mathematical activities in focus at P2

1. They participate in exploring, showing anticipation and appropriate responses to familiar people, activities and routines.
2. They have become involved, actively explore and manipulate objects, remember and apply potential solutions. They communicate choices, likes and dislikes using sounds, tones and/or gestures as they move towards gaining skills that will support understanding.

EQUALS Level 3 • Varied deliberate reactions – Imitate gestures and activities, recognise cause and effect/explore associate properties. Anticipate events.

Key levels of experience
• Participation
• Involvement
• Understanding

**P3. Practical examples**

• Collecting items together – this can occur as part of a game played with a group, for example collecting the items they knock over with a swinging ball, or collecting tokens you give them if they manage to score by landing a ball rolled down a piece of plastic drain pipe into a bucket.

• A line of five small drawers each labelled with a number 1 to 5 can be used in many ways, for example as a number line for putting items in sequentially. This equipment plays on children's natural fascination with drawers, finding out what's inside, putting things in and taking things out. They provide useful concrete experiences of object permanence, visualisation, itemisation, partitioning, and sequential increase/decrease of quantity. Though some aspects of experience that occur with line drawers such as number names, numeral recognition, name order, naming quantities, addition etc. may be beyond the child's present abilities, they are still valuable incidental experiences.

• Use a row of big mac speaking switches, with one, two and three programmed on them, for choice making or prediction activities, for example roll big dice, choose the mac with the same pattern, or choose the mac that will say how many sweets are on the table. Adult support will differentiate the task to promote appropriate success, although it should be recognised that failing or scoring nothing is a valuable learning experience.

## Strands of the Numeracy Strategy

| Strand description<br>• Reception<br>• Y1 onwards | Counting and recognising numbers<br>The number system | Adding and subtracting<br>Calculations | Solving problems<br>Handling data | Measures,<br>shape and space |
|---|---|---|---|---|
| Interpretation that describes the strand appropriately for PLD pupils | Appreciating quantity.<br>*Noticing, itemising, identifying, matching.* | Appreciating and anticipating changes that create increase and decrease.<br>*Collecting, separating. Precursors to calculating.* | Active responses – making things happen. Organising responses, things and information.<br>*Comparing and remembering. Precursors to recording.* | Appreciating and manipulating space, shape and time patterns. |
| *Teaching Focus*<br>**Sensory Development Including Attention and Perception** | Scan, anticipate and make choices about stimulus and objects. Recognise and make sense of incomplete or partially hidden object, or image. Use pattern recognition (subitising) to recognise there are differences in small groups 1 to 4. Selectively maintain attention or switch attention as appropriate. Connect between different representations of same item, e.g. real object/image/name. | Recognise connections between stimuli/objects/events. Engage in close attention to changing quantities and anticipate changes. Discriminate (by subitising) between small groups (1 to 4), recognising more/less, choose group with most. Maintain interest in quantities after they have been hidden. Appreciate when there are still more hidden items yet to be revealed. | Exercise choice and control, making selections about changing stimuli. Discriminate differences and make connections between objects. Relate the use of objects to appropriate events. Anticipate identity of partially hidden objects. Identify functional side of object. Use specific eye pointing to objects in sequence, forward and back. | Associate objects of similar shapes together – equate to representation. Anticipate and respond appropriately to spaces shapes, patterns of time and to changes in position, size, etc. Discern odd one out, etc. Make choices about them and show preferences. Make decisions about direction and movement. Make large exploratory movements feeling objects/space. |
| **Active Physical Development** | Show deliberate intent. Choose and obtain objects. Place items in receptacles one at once. Use rhythmic sequences, touching, pointing, picking and moving objects in turn. Point at marks. Coordinate sound making to pointing. | Gather collections and separate groups of items. Experience incremental itemisation of objects, or on a physical number line/string. Participate with adult itemising objects. Make sound or rhythm to itemise up and down – include nothing left. Tally objects/events using fingers and sounds (up and down) – accompany adult number names. Make sounds and gestures to symbolise none, one, and more, here and gone. | Actively instigate changes to objects and collections, events, etc. Create effect by moving/positioning objects. Experience various schema as appropriate, e.g. vertical/horizontal, circular, trajectory, enclosure, rotation, etc. Anticipate effects – change of place, increase or depletion, etc. Integrate picking and placing schema to place items next to each other. Combine objects appropriately. Point to marks – make marks. | Participate and experiment with changing positions of objects. Anticipate effects of changes of shape and size. Explore bringing shapes together and creating sequences of shapes, objects or sounds – vocal or instrumental. Choose spaces to move to or be in. Experiment with changing body position, posture, movement, direction, speed, rhythm, etc. |
| **Sharing and Communicating** | Initiate and take turns communicating about quantities, imitating gestures and sounds. Respond to object or event names appropriately. Appreciate meaning of 'objects of reference'. Ask for items that are not in sight – by any means of communication. Coordinate sound making with rhythmic gestures/pointing. Appreciate adult use of number names during the itemising process, and in the description of quantity. | Offer and accept items. Showing items to gain attention or giving items to prompt actions. Use own personal sounds, symbols or gestures to name objects, events or numbers. Itemise using sequences of sounds. Use intonation to mark beginning/end. Ask for items that are out of sight. Use deferral imitation – copying the actions of a person who is not present. | Express desire to change stimuli/event or objects. Anticipate and respond to instructions, e.g. wait 1, 2, 3, now. Use own personal sounds, intonations, and gestures to indicate objects, actions and to instigate and direct events. Anticipate and express consequences of change. Direct a sequence of events. Take items and place in organised ways. | Share attention about shape, space, size, and time. Take turns in communications about them. Use gesture vocalisation and tones that relate to size, frequency, duration, etc. Adopt consistent name sounds or signs for places, shapes, dimensions, actions, etc. Refer to objects and places that are not present. |

Most learning activities will include a variety of elements of focus

**Figure 13.9** Mathematical activities in focus at P3

which is to devise practical ideas for lessons that include the activities. Some illustrations of practical applications are included in panels. Two books rich in practical ideas are Judy Davis (2001) and Flo Longhorn (2000)

## Delivering the curriculum

### Using National Numeracy Strategy planning

It is useful to use the overall structure of the National Numeracy Strategy long term planning frameworks to outline weekly coverage, because they maintain percentages of time to be spent on basic and supplementary skills. They also ensure the revisiting aspects or 'topics', which is proven to be an effective way of embedding and reinforcing learning. It is however useful to adapt the given format and add a qualifying description in the topic column, which describes your special interpretation of the strand or topic as appropriate to pupils need. E.g. where the topic is Counting, insert – *appreciating quantity (for other suggestions see Figure 13.5).*

It was originally suggested that where all pupils are working below level one it would be appropriate to use the Reception year teaching programme. However in accord with the 2001 guidelines to promote a climate of progression through school it would be constructive to adapt the chronologically appropriate planner or key stage framework. This will help ensure that some themes such as fractions, proportion, handling data, algebra, etc. are approached albeit through accessible practical interpretation and application. Planning may be done either by importing references into the topic column of Reception Year Planner to create a modified version, (with qualifying descriptions as above). Or by interpreting the fundamental sense of the content described in the age appropriate year planner, and devising objectives at suitable levels for the students. Such modifications can be noted in the Objectives column of the year planner, e.g. *Multiplication* in Year 5 may be experienced by *'Accumulating repeating collections'*. Or *Handling data* might be reinterpreted as *'Putting things in order or representing information'*, an example might be keeping tally in games or events etc. The new guidelines for access to the National Curriculum promote such modifications, supporting the ideal of providing opportunities and activities at each key stage, that relate back to fundamental learning experiences. The intended supplements of examples from the Numeracy Strategy will also support such processes. Though all should emphasise the need to ensure that activities are relevant to pupils lives and avoid tokenism.

It is possible that once long term plans are outlined for each key stage they can stand as a reference which teachers use as the start of their planning process for a period of years subject to periodic review.

Ann Berger and colleagues (2000) reduced medium term planning to a minimum outlining the terms work under headings of Topic and Objectives as taken from the long term planner, but allowing for noting some variation or customisation to meet immediate circumstances.

Short term plans require more detail though a weekly format with a row for each day, and column for each part of the lesson can be adequate. The starting points for short term planning are key objectives from the medium term plan. In addition it is useful to note the specific or sub-objectives, tasks/activities, and any particular support or differentiation strategies. Notes on grouping/staffing, may sometimes be pertinent and it can be helpful to outline key vocabulary or questions used. Two columns on the reverse of the sheet can be used for evaluation and outlook, commenting on any aspects of the lesson or achievements, and noting ideas about next steps, targets or homework, which may be encouraging parental support in practical activities.

## The daily maths lesson

The benefits of a daily lesson of mathematics are a central principle of the Numeracy Strategy. For groups of pupils with special needs the daily lesson should be as long as is sensible to meet their needs, there may be many variations in the structure of the lessons, it is underlying learning principles that are important.

Each part of the recommended three part lesson structure suggested in the framework, oral mental starter, main activities and plenary has a valuable part to play, but can be interpreted flexibly. For example an oral mental starter may be used to remind, direct, and share focus and be followed by short exploratory or practising task for individuals or groups supported by adults. After which children may be drawn back for another chunk of direct teaching, followed by another practical spell etc. So the parts are broken into chunks that match children's concentration or support needs. With some classes such an approach might be unduly disruptive or organisationally difficult and adapting teaching strategies within a more continuous structure would be preferred. Judy Davis (2001) discusses incorporating specific maths targets into a range of activities in chapter seven of her book.

It may not always be apt to include a plenary with every lesson, but it is desirable to ensure that at some time in the week there is a session that allows opportunities for reinforcement, motivating children by praise, or encouraging the demonstration of skills they have been practising. These strategies remind children of what they have been learning about and look forward to future experiences. For some pupils one approach to such a session could be a memory box or bag with items from the lessons, with others it may be achieved by emphasising and reminding them about the maths experienced in practical sessions, e.g. if they made pizza, as they share it out and eat it.

The National Numeracy Strategy emphasises the power of children working together expressing or demonstrating their own skills and understandings and the value of modelling language for them, but it should also be recognised that when working with children who have learning and communication difficulties teachers and support assistants may have special roles in modelling, supporting and complementing children's participation. The elements of direct teaching as described in section one of the framework can be adopted and interpreted as appropriate to the needs of the pupils, they are:

1. Instruction or direction.

2. Demonstration and modelling.

3. Explaining and illustrating.

4. Questioning – which may include 'show me'.

5. Consolidation, practice and reinforcement.

6. Use of skills beyond mathematics lessons.

7. Evaluating children's responses.

8. Summarising key ideas.

*Differentiation*

In mixed ability classes children of different abilities may draw different learning from the same activities. Well-judged use of the elements of direct teaching described above may contribute to such differentiation. For example within a dice game, it might be appropriate for one pupil to have skills like pointing and itemising targeted and for adults to provide the vocalisation of number names, or assist the precision movement of his counters that helps him participate with the other pupils, who are involved at higher levels, identifying quantities etc. There are a variety of ways to provide differentiation:

- **Differentiation by task**. Which might be achieved in different ways. For example, different outcomes may be expected from the same task, or children may start on different steps of the task, or there may be separate tasks though they relate to a common theme.
- **Differentiation by support**. Individuals or groups within groups may be supported by prompts, pointers focusing attention, demonstration or modelling alternative language or signs and symbols etc.
- **Differentiation through resources**. Concrete apparatus or objects, tallies, number lines, collecting boxes etc. High-tech or low-tech communication aids, IT access devices, aids to manipulation, aids for sensory impairment.

## Adopting age appropriate approaches

It is recognised that particularly with PLD students whose progression is predominantly lateral there must be differentiation providing age appropriate activities and equipment that support learning themes drawn from early key stages. For example for teenagers who are using single switch or simple choice computer programs you may wish to use images of themselves or friends, pop stars or footballers instead of the teddies or infant friendly graphics usually found in early years software. Custom programs can be devised using Microsoft PowerPoint, and the mouse can be modified to take the switch jack. Use real things to count, e.g. household items, a collection of lipsticks or nail varnishes, local football team replicas. Magazines and shopping catalogues, even junk mail provide many age appropriate images for collecting, counting making graphs etc. It is surprising how much more motivating real objects are than special counting equipment. Often items like kitchen brushes, personal care items, sports and leisure goods, or novelty items like witches finger extensions available at Halloween, have attractive sensory dimensions that make children want to manipulate them. They offer opportunities to count, match and control quantities that students will relish. When used well boxes, containers and bags stimulate pupils curiosity, and offer a wide range of opportunities to illustrate concepts like object permanence, collecting, addition to multiplication etc. The humble egg box is a powerful means of demonstrating number patterns (subitising), it can be used to reveal and conceal patterns, challenging visualisation and illustrating conservation. For those of you who are faint-hearted plastic eggs can be purchased from craft shops. So the daily lesson does not have to use mathematical resources from educational catalogues, and the mathematical activities in the lesson do not have to be abstract. Almost any game of chance or manipulation requiring scoring can be turned to the purpose of a daily maths lesson, exploiting the need for the language of turns and sequences, tracking, manipulating and communicating about quantities, and much more.

Tokens, collecting trays, tally sticks, tally beads, marker sheets, plastic numerals, fridge magnets etc, can all be used to extend the tactile experience of cumulative scoring, and provide more learning tasks within the activity. You set the level of challenge and adapt the game to match circumstances the students needs.

We should also recognise that counting and fundamental mathematics are practical, and using them in practical circumstances is an avenue that can provide both age appropriate opportunities and motivation. The practical use of maths skills are valid components of the daily lesson, e.g. an enormous amount of mathematical operations and language, offering a variety of levels of participation will be entered into if we take ingredients and make a pizza, or omelette, indeed such lessons are so rich in potential that they could be repeated a number of times exploiting different mathematical themes each time. The important thing to bear in mind is that the mathematical communication within the process must be exploited, because that is the purpose of the lesson; the product is the motivational bonus. So it may be quite appropriate for the adult to do many of the processes, e.g. chopping the onion, and make sure that the mathematical language and experiences, e.g. half, quarter etc. are being emphasised.

This book has been a journey through early learning, it may have taught you nothing new, because repeatedly it focuses on how much we take for granted, it has been full of little aspects of learning that are so important. Remember maths is all around us, even in the rhythm of our heart. It is our job to fascinate our pupils so that they are keen to find out about quantities, space and time, it shouldn't be difficult because they have an inbuilt fascination for these things, so go on make it live.

# References

Aarons, M. and Gittens, T. (1999) *The Handbook of Autism*. London: Routledge.

Banes, D. (1999) *Spiral Mathematics*. Tamworth: NASEN.

Berger, A., Morris, D. and Portman, J. (2000) *Implementing the National Numeracy Strategy for Pupils with Learning Difficulties*. London: David Fulton Publishers.

Brown, E. (1996) *Religious Education for All*. London: David Fulton Publishers.

Butterworth, B. (1999) *What Counts*. New York: The Free Press.

Butterworth, G. (1998) 'What is special about pointing in babies', in Simion, F. and Butterworth, G. (eds) *The Development of Sensory, Motor, and Cognitive Capacities in Early Infancy*. Hove: UK Psychology Press.

Cavigioli, O. and Reynolds, B. (1999) 'Aiming true', *Special Children* **116**, January.

Chugani, H. T. and Phelps, M. E. (1986) 'Maturation changes in cerebral function in infants determined by FDG positron emission tomography', *Science* **231**, 840–3.

Davis, J. (2001) *A Sensory Approach to the Curriculum*. London: David Fulton Publishers.

Dehaene, S. (1997) *The Number Sense*. USA: Oxford University Press.

Dehaene, S. (1999) *The Number Sense*, 80–8, 92–5. London: Penguin.

DeLoache, J. S. (1987) 'Rapid change in the symbolic functioning of very young children', *Science* **238**, 1556–7.

Dodd, G. H. (1989) 'Aromacology'. Paper delivered at British Psychological Society conference, London. December.

Donaldson, M. (1978) *Children's Minds*. London: Fontana.

Donaldson, M. (1979) 'The mismatch between school and children's minds', *Human Nature*, March, 60–7.

Dunn, J. (1988) *The Beginnings of Social Understanding*. Oxford: Blackwell.

Einstein, A. 'Letter to J. Hadamard', in Hadamard, J. *The Psychology of Invention in the Mathematical Field*. Princeton University Press.

EQUALS (1998) *Baseline assessment and curriculum target setting for access to the National Curriculum*. Tyne & Wear: EQUALS.

EQUALS (1999) *Schemes of work for mathematics: SLD, PLD, MLD*. Tyne & Wear: EQUALS.

Fuson, K. C. and Hall, J. W. (1983) 'The acquisition of early number word meanings. A conceptual analysis and review', in Ginsburg, H. P. (ed.) *The Development of Mathematical Thinking*. New York: Academic Press.

Fuson, K. C., Richards, J. and Moser, J. M. (1982) 'The acquisition and elaboration of the number word sequence', in Brainerd, C. *Progress in Cognitive Development: Children's logical and mathematical cognition*, vol. 1. New York: Springer Verlag.

Galanter, E. (1962) 'Contemporary psychophysics', in Brown, R. *et al.* (eds) *New Directions in Psychology*, 153. New York: Rinehard & Winston.

Geary, D. C. (1994) *Children's Mathematical Development: Research and practical applications*. Washington, DC: American Psychological Association.

Gelman, R. (1979) 'Preschool thought', *American Psychologist* **34**, 900–5.

Gelman, R. and Gallistel, R. C. (1978) *The Child's Understanding of Number*. Cambridge, Mass.: Harvard University Press.

Gelman, R. and Meck, E. (1983) 'Preschoolers counting: principles before skills', *Cognition* **13**, 343–59.

Gibson, E. J. and Walk, R. D. (1960) 'The visual cliff', *Scientific American*, April, 64–71 and 193.

Gregory, R. L. and Wallace, J. G. (1963) 'Recovery from early blindness'. Experimental Psychology Society Monographs. No. 2.

Grove, N. and Peacy, N. (1999) 'Teaching subjects to pupils with profound learning difficulties', *British Journal of Special Education* **26**, 2.

Hendrickson, H. and McLinden, M. (1977) 'Implications of a visual impairment for early communication development', *The SLD Experience*, Issue 17, Kidderminster.

Hughes, M. (1986) *Children and Number*. Oxford: Blackwell.

Hughes, M. and Grieve, R. (1980) 'On asking children bizarre questions', *First Language*, 146–60.

Longhorn, F. (1988) *A Sensory Curriculum for Very Special People*. London: Souvenir Press.

Longhorn, F. (2000) *Numeracy for Very Special People*. Wooton, Bedfordshire: Catalyst.

Luria, A. R. (1961) *The Role of Speech in the Regulation of Normal and Abnormal Behaviour*. Oxford: Pergamon.

McEvoy, J. (1989) 'From counting to arithmetic', *British Journal of Special Education* **16**, 3, Research Supplement, 107–10.

Miller, G. A. (1956) 'The magical number 7 + or – 2' *Psychological Review* **63**, 81–97.

Munn, P. (1997) 'Children's beliefs about counting', in Thompson, I. (ed.) *Teaching and Learning Early Number*, 9–19. Buckingham, Philadelphia: Open University Press.

Neisser, U. (1976) *Cognition and Reality*. San Francisco: W. H. Freeman.

Nelson, K. (1973) 'Structure and strategy in learning to talk'. Society for research into child development monographs, 149, Nos 1 and 2. Yale University.

Nielsen, L. (1987) *Spatial Relations in Congenitally Blind Infants*. Kalundbork, Denmark: Refnarskolen.

Nutbrown, C. (1999) *Threads of Thinking*. London: Paul Chapman.

Park, K. (1997) 'Loitering within tent', *The SLD Experience*, Issue 18, Kidderminster.

Piaget, J. (1965) *The Child's Conception of Number*. London: Routledge and Kegan Paul.

Piaget, J. and Inhelder, B. (1969) *The Psychology of the Child*. London: Routledge and Kegan Paul.

PIVATS (2000) *Performance Indicators for Value Added Target Setting*. Preston: Lancashire County Council.

QCA (1998) *Supporting the Target Setting Process – Guidance for effective target setting for pupils with special educational needs*, Ref. STSSS. Sudbury: DfEE Publications.

QCA (1999) *Shared World, Different Experiences – Designing the curriculum for pupils who are deafblind*. Sudbury: DfEE Publications.

QCA (2001) *Planning, teaching and assessing the curriculum for pupils with learning difficulties*. Sudbury: DfEE.

Quinn, B. and Malone, A. (2000) *Pervasive Developmental Disorder: an altered perspective*. London: Jessica Kingsley.

SCAA (1996) *Planning the Curriculum for Pupils with Profound and Multiple Learning Difficulties*. London: SCAA.

Schaffer, B., Eggleston, V. H. and Scott, J. C. (1974) 'Number development in young children', *Cognitive Psychology* **6**, 357–79.

Segall, M. H. *et al.* (1990) *Human Behaviour in Global Perspective: An introduction to cross cultural psychology*. New York: Pergamon.

Shepard, R. N. (1990) *Mind Sights*. New York: Freeman.

Siegel, L. S. and Hodkin, B. (1982) 'The garden path to the understanding of cognitive development: has Piaget lead us into the poison ivy', in Modgil, S. and Modgil, C. (eds) *Jean Piaget Consensus and Controversy*. New York: Preager.

Skills Factory (2000) *Numeracy Complete*. Uppermill, Saddleworth OL3 6FF. The Skills Factory.

Starkey, P., Spelke, E. S. and Gelman, R. (1983) 'Detection of intermodal numerical correspondances by human infants', *Science* **222**, 179–81.

Staves, L. (2000) 'Looking into the levels', *Special Children* **129**, 24–8.

Turnbull, C. (1961) *The Forest People*, New York: Simon and Schuster.

Uzgiris, I. C. and Hunt, J. McVoy (1975) *Assessment in Infancy: Ordinal scales of psychological development*. University of Illinois Press.

Vygotsky, L. S. (1932, reprinted 1962) *Thought and Language*. Cambridge, Mass.: MIT Press.

Williams, D. (1992) *Nobody Nowhere*. London: Doubleday. (Also published by Corgi, 1993)

Wragg, E. C. (1997) *The Cubic Curriculum*. London: Routledge.

Wynn, K. (1992) 'Addition and subtraction by human infants', *Nature* **358**, 749–59.

# Index